MARRIAGE
AND
FAMILY

MARRIAGE AND FAMILY

*Relics of the Past
or Promise of the Future?*

Edited and with an
Introduction by
George Augustin

Paulist Press
New York/Mahwah, NJ

Cover and book design by Sharyn Banks

Copyright © 2015 by the Kardinal Walter Kasper Instituts für Theologie, Ökumene und Spiritualität

Library of Congress Control Number: 2015946953

ISBN 978-0-8091-4972-8 (paperback)
ISBN 978-1-58768-598-9 (e-book)

Published by Paulist Press
997 Macarthur Boulevard
Mahwah, New Jersey 07430

www.paulistpress.com
Printed and bound in the United States of America

CONTENTS

∽

v

INTRODUCTION

⌘

With the announcement of the synods of bishops, 2014–2015, Pope Francis has once again placed the theme "marriage and family" at the center of ecclesial attention. As if tuning the orchestra in preparation for the synod, Cardinal Walter Kasper, at the pope's invitation, in February 2014 pronounced a much-commented-upon discourse before the Consistory of Cardinals on the subject "The gospel of the family." Thereupon was ignited a somewhat turbulent discussion. With the present volume, titled *Marriage and Family*, we wish to examine the issues of this discussion, set forth the problems of marriage and family in the contemporary world, and contribute to a better and more profound comprehension of Church doctrine concerning this theme.

The results of the presynod poll on the situation of the family, carried out on a global scale by the Roman secretariat for the synod, made clear that there are great differences, in the context of the universal Church, between ecclesial doctrine and praxis with respect to marriage and family. It turns out that doctrine and life are notably far apart from each other. Here it is necessary to ask, How can we newly reconcile life and doctrine and overcome the existing discrepancy?

In a globalized and pluralist world, the Church, as a worldwide community of testimony and faith, lives in an environment of great tension due to the asynchrony of cultures.

This asynchrony, this difference in the rhythm of cultural development, affects the perception of the contents and the praxis of the faith. Hence, in seeking pastoral solutions for the configuration of marriage and the family, we must keep sight of anthropological and sociocultural factors and interpret the vital reality of believers in the light of the gospel.

This can be achieved only by taking seriously the reality of people's lives. For this, faith must be perceived as the basis for action and as an aid in orientation for praxis. It is the Church's responsibility to continually clarify the existential meaning of her doctrine and to motivate people to realize the message of the gospel in their practical life. Starting from the spirit of the gospel and from the values cemented in it, we Christians have the task of making present the holiness of marriage and of the family, and defending them against danger.

It is a permanent challenge to clarify and explain that Christian morality is not a morality of prohibitions, but promise and orientation to life in its fullness (John 10:10). To be Christian means to be able, with the grace of God, to cooperate with total confidence and live in the following of Christ. Christian morality is a morality of impulse and of service to life: it is, at bottom, a morality of capacitation.

A Christian morality without theological depth and spiritual breadth becomes irrelevant in the short term, without doubt, and cannot serve Christian and human growth in society. The Church, if she wants to be equal to her worldwide responsibility, has to adopt a critical-positive position before the secularized world, even in matters of the ethical ordering of society.

In this aspect, it is the task of the Church to announce in a comforting and intelligible way, in the heart of a transformed social situation, the message, based on the gospel of Jesus Christ, of the beauty and the value of marriage and family. It has to be clear: the Church wants to serve the life and the love of the people. The Church wants the life of marriages and families to be truly achieved. In all practical applications of doctrine, this fundamental intention can and must be clearly recognizable.

Today, this positive message of the Church does not reach, for different reasons, many believers. On the one hand, they don't see the intention of the ecclesial doctrine concerning marriage and family to serve life; on the other, the relevant aspects for life in the doctrine of the Church are not communicated clearly, synthetically, and intelligibly.

We cannot nor is it permissible for us to change the content and substance of the biblical message to suit our taste. Instead of this, we are to seek pathways, to see how we may win people over and awaken their enthusiasm for the message. It's a matter of making manifest how the richness and grandeur of Church doctrine concerning life and love in marriage and family can be experienced and developed. The transmission of the gospel of marriage and family has to regain a high pastoral priority and become a missionary concern for all believers.

Regarding this, we have to move past fixation on singular problematic themes and present anew and in a positive way the meaning and the aim of Church doctrine. Our main concern should be not to lose ourselves in particular theological and casuistic discussions, but with all zeal to openly communicate the meaning of the Catholic idea of marriage. A change of perspectives and of paradigms is necessary. Our focus must be on the fulfilled life of marriage and family.

A multitude of questions arise: How can we strengthen marriage and family in their multiple challenges? What can we do, personally and as Church, to create the conditions in which people can, full of confidence, with complete responsibility and in the awareness of God's loving presence, structure their marital and family life?

We are not spared the struggle to seek, from the spirit of the gospel, answers to pressing questions about marriage and family. It is a matter of seeking pathways for announcing the gospel of marriage and family in our diverse society, in such a way that people understand it not as a prohibition or impediment to life, but rather as an indicator toward the configuration of a fulfilled life. We are to pastorally convey the theological idea of marriage and family in a way that can be beneficial to the daily reality of marriage and family.

The Church, as community of faith, must be consequently willing to accept and bear with all humility that we cannot find a satisfactory solution for all problems, including for those that concern marriage and family. The believer has no choice but to face these contradictions of life with the experience of the cross of the Lord. Here a reciprocal effect is reached. The Christian idea of marriage and family presupposes the general human idea. The Christian raises the human to a divine level, which is grace and capacity. As Christians we are urged to seek in common pathways to a regained awareness of the social, philosophical, and theological foundation of marriage and the family. According to the Catholic idea, marriage is a community of life and love between a man and a woman, freely accepted for one's whole life and sanctioned by sacrament, that is ordered to the mutual well-being of the couple and the generation and education of the offspring. The family is where we experience the dignity of each individual as well as the entirety of human culture. Here people learn—both parents and children—the practice of compassion and love of neighbor. The future of humanity depends decisively on the stability and framework of values of the families.

As a permanent task of theological reflection and pastoral announcement, we recognize the need to clarify time and again that the Christian vision of marriage and family responds to the profound longing of the human heart. In the light of Christian faith, this allows the love between man and woman, parents and children, to shine with new splendor.

Experience shows that the traditional and uncontaminated family offers children the most secure and suitable environment. It collaborates in their integral development. Children who grow up with their biological parents, married to each other, have the best possibilities for a harmonic development of their personality. They run the least risk of having negative experiences in the family environment. This is confirmed by sociological investigations in all the cultures of the world. The Church moves in this ambience of experience and takes up the desire to light the way for people to be able to dominate, with the strength of God, the many challenges of marriage and family life. She makes her own the genuinely human longing for stability and security and accompanies people in the diverse phases of life and in its different tasks, enabling them to be good spouses and responsible and loving progenitors. For children and youth the Church sees herself as an important interlocutor and traveling companion.

This, together with fundamental attitudes and ideals, demands answers to well-defined questions. The question about a high divorce rate and its long-term effects for society must be addressed. Do we, as Christians, have to accept it as inevitable fatality? What can we do to avoid, in the spirit of Jesus Christ, the multiple motives that lead to divorce and overcome them through the practice of reconciliation and mercy? On this point, the much-argued problem of admitting communion to the civilly divorced and remarried will not occupy the first place. It is rather a matter of the fundamental concern: What can we do, on a purely practical plane, from the spirit of Jesus Christ, in order that marriages and families continue to be fulfilled today?

Married couples who dedicate themselves to living a Christian marriage know that the road of matrimony is not easy. But if this road is traveled with the strength of God, it can be fulfilling in itself and overflow with blessings for the marriage and the family.

The main challenge, then, for pastoral activity today is this: How can we ourselves attain to the conviction that the Catholic doctrine of marriage and family is not some outdated concept of the distant past but the promise of true human happiness, developed from the plenitude of faith and, at the same time, made possible by grace?

The sacrament of matrimony is the permanent source of grace, bringing strength to daily marital life by structuring the community of life and love between woman and man. This grace carries the strength to forgive and forget. The sacrament helps each overcome selfish interests, solve of conflicts in the spirit of Christ, and cooperate so that both may grow.

The authors of this thematic volume each contribute their own perspective to develop an updated spirituality of marriage and family—nourished by the depth of the Catholic faith—and thereby produce a timely discussion that presents the challenges of pastoral activity for marriage and family. They are united in the desire to seek answers to the distinct problems in keeping with the gospel and the Spirit of Christ. We thank all of the people who have cooperated in this work, above all the authors and the translators and the Loyola Communications Group for their cordial and efficient collaboration.

The doctrine of the Church concerning marriage and family does not represent some specialized morality but is intended for all men and women of good will. It arises from reflection on divine and human life. It grows with the deepening and development of the moral sense, already inscribed in Creation, and that, with the revelation of God in the history of salvation, experiences his outpouring of grace. It is a permanent task to theoretically reexamine, in light of the diverse situations of people's lives, this foundation of Christian life in its relevance for the fulfillment of marriage and family life, and put it within reach of all as orientation, as a mobilizing motive, and as a source of productive energy. Where people embrace it as a foundation in their own lives, marriages, and families, it brings a culture of love to fruition. Here, man and woman, parents and children jointly display care for one another and mutually relate with respect and gratitude. Here develops a culture of love that is beautiful and true, life affirming and promoting, at once divine and human.

Vallendar, on the Feast of the Assumption of Mary,
15th of August, 2014

1

THE DEVOLUTION OF AN AMERICAN CATHOLIC FAMILY

From Piety to Pluralism in Four Generations

TERRENCE KEELEY

⁂

The General Synod of October 2015 for pastoral challenges to the family in the context of evangelization faces daunting tasks. Over the past half-century, traditional Church teachings and modern, familial practice have sharply diverged. By the end of this decade, less than one-third of the children in Western cultures will be raised in traditional nuclear families; children born out of wedlock, separated from their parents by divorce or immigration, orphaned or brought up in a same-sex marriage will outnumber those living with both of their biological parents by a two-to-one margin. Church efforts to advance the proven successes of nuclear families are failing. Similarly, dwindling numbers of Catholics pay heed to the Church's teaching on sex.[1] Attitudes among practicing Catholics towards birth control are well-known; Church doctrine is widely ignored. According to the Pew Research Center's 2013 Global Survey, moreover, homosexuality has become broadly accepted in North America, the European

Union, and much of Latin America. Alongside these trends the Church's own moral authority has been cast in doubt. Over the past decade, thousands of clergymen have been disciplined for sexual improprieties against children.[2] These scandals have gravely tarnished the Church's image and given voice to a debilitating accusation: *hypocrisy*. Family-centered exhortations such as those in *Familiaris Consortio*, *Gaudium et Spes*, and Pope Francis's most recent, *Evangelii Gaudium*, contain great wisdom. Still, no organization can lead its followers or inspire others when its own leaders have repeatedly failed to practice what they have solemnly pledged.

> *The essence and role of the family are, in the final analysis, specified by love.*
>
> *The family has the mission to guard, reveal and communicate love.*
>
> *John Paul II*
> Familiaris Consortio

My own upbringing could not have been more Catholic. My parents remained together for fifty-three years, until my mother's death. They raised eight children—my five brothers, two sisters, and me. All of us were baptized, attended church regularly, practiced the sacraments, and went to Catholic schools for at least part of our education. Two of us attended the University of Notre Dame, perhaps the world's premiere Catholic institute of higher learning. Five of us married, two of us to practicing Catholics. We now have our own children, a new generation of eight daughters and three sons. In their adulthoods, three of my brothers confirmed they were gay. Two now have committed partners. My fifteen direct cousins brought another twenty-nine souls into the world. For reasons that will be made clear, however, the gift of Catholic faith has not been widely retained or broadly transmitted to the youngest generation. Indeed, despite their deep and inspirational Catholic piety, less than one-quarter of my grandparent's descendants and their chosen partners are practicing Catholics today. The story of how our collective religious beliefs and practices have evolved over the past seven decades speaks directly to the challenges and opportunities the General Synod has been called to address.

OUR LADY OF THE ASSUMPTION

My grandparents—Richard William and Theresa Canny Keeley, and Hector and Solange Gougeon Malette—were models of Catholic devotion and practice. The former were both born in Connecticut, where their parents had settled after emigrating from County Offaly, Ireland in the late nineteenth century. The first Mallet came to Ville Marie (today, Montreal) with Maisonneuve in the 1640s.[3] Killeigh, Ireland—the village in Offaly where Keeleys are originally from—means "church in the field." Solange means "only angel" in French. As fate would have it, Dick and Tess Keeley, and Hector and Solange Malette ultimately settled and raised their families near the U.S. border, in Windsor, Ontario.

My father had one sister; my mother four sisters and two brothers. All of my aunts and uncles attended Catholic schools, mostly in Windsor. The sisters at St. Clare's Grade School and St. Mary's High School, as well as the Basilian fathers at Assumption High School, played prominent roles in their formation.

*As living members of the family, children contribute in
their own way to making their parents holy.*

Paul VI
Gaudium et Spes

My paternal grandfather was active in the Knights of
Columbus. He was himself ultimately honored twice, as a
Knight of St. Gregory as well as a Knight of Malta. His life
was one of unwavering devotion to Catholic causes—chairing
the boards of the local Catholic university and hospital, the
Rosary Campaign, First Friday Club, and the construction of
residences for unwed mothers. His son—my father—was an
altar boy, as well as a self-described mute in the church choir.
After the guns of World War II quieted, Papa—as we called
my father's father—received communion daily. His role in
leading a large munitions factory to support the Allied effort
likely contributed both to his sense of communal duty as well
as his appreciation for the temporality of life.

Hector Malette was a communitarian too, one who
worked quietly and tirelessly behind the scenes. He studied
pharmacology and established his own pharmaceutical business catering to Hotel Dieu, the largest Catholic hospital in
Windsor. Hector had four brothers and six sisters, all born in
Wendover, Ontario. His father was a blacksmith who died in
his early forties. His mother subsequently moved to Ottawa
and took in boarders. Hector's brother Eugene entered the
Frères Ecole Chrétien in Laval, Quebec at age thirteen and
remained a Catholic brother all his life. After some years in the
seminary, Hector left the religious life. "I recall seeing my
Dad and Mom kneeling beside their bed praying silently, and
alone at times, in the morning and at night," my Aunt Sue
reports. Aunt Sue herself entered the convent at age seven-

teen, the only vocation in this tale. She has since spent fifty-seven years of vowed life in the Congregation of the Sisters of the Holy Names of Jesus and Mary. At this writing, my father and Aunt Sue are the only survivors of the second generation.

As a pharmacist, Hector Malette was frequently called late in the night to render a service for a sick child or adult needing immediate medication. Whenever one of the parents of the Sisters of the Holy Names became gravely ill, Grandpapa would dutifully drive them three or more hours away to be reunited, always at night after working on his feet all day at the pharmacy. He and Solange would not have thought to send their seven children to anything other than Catholic schools. Solange also attended Mass frequently, daily even during Lent and Advent. The Immaculate Conception, Our Lady of Guadalupe, and Our Lady of the Assumption parishes were all within walking distance of Malette homes, intentionally. As a young family, the Malettes prayed the rosary together daily after supper dishes had been put away. Every Malette wedding took place in Catholic parishes in Windsor, even those where the spouses were Protestant or Jewish.

> *The Church has a single intention: that God's kingdom may come, and that the salvation of the whole human race may come to pass.*
>
> *Paul VI*
> Gaudium et Spes

When Richard Keeley and Denise Malette wed at Our Lady of the Assumption on September 20, 1952, one thing was beyond question: they would remain faithful to their Catholic roots. As they moved their ever-growing family to five different American states and one Canadian province in search of economic opportunity, they diligently sought out their local parish priest to make sure their children had exposure to parochial schools, even if only for catechism lessons. Settling finally in Adrian, Michigan, our family grew particularly close to the Adrian Dominican Sisters and Siena Heights College, which the sisters run. Following in his father's footsteps, my father founded the St. Mary's Parish Council and later chaired the board of trustees at Siena Heights. "From the late 1970s until today," my father says, "my closest friends have been Dominican sisters."

In addition to my mother, two other Malettes married Catholics: John to Mary Bridgeman, and Claude to Gloria Sendlack. Remarkably, all of the practicing Catholics in the Keeley/Malette families today emanate from these three marriages *alone*. Indeed, only one of every eight descendants and partners of my other aunts and uncles today even consider themselves Christian, let alone practicing Catholics.[4] To remain alive, it seems, Catholicism needs both parents to remain active practitioners—and even that may not suffice.

DOUBTS, DISSENT AND DEMONS

The Keeley children grew up to be independent thinkers. In his mid-teens, after hours of thoughtful debate about Church doctrine with Fr. Roger Stanley of St. Mary's Parish, my eldest brother Michael asked my parents for permission to attend other religious services. My father, who enjoyed spirited, respectful dialogue due in part to his Jesuit training, said he could as long as he dressed properly, stayed for the entire service, and contributed to the collection basket. "I never developed a personal relationship with Jesus," Michael now says, "but I was moved by how images drawn from his teaching helped frame purposeful lives." For a time at the University of Notre Dame, Michael contemplated the priesthood. He went on to become a Peace Corps volunteer in the Philippines, and has spent the bulk of his professional career in public service, creating among other things more than twelve thousand charter school seats for underprivileged minority youth in Los Angeles County.

Of my five brothers and two sisters, only two were never confirmed: my sister Carol and brother Mark. Carol recalls the sober conversation with my father that led to her decision:

> "As I understand it, confirmation is like baptism, only I am choosing for myself rather than you choosing for me." That's right, Dad said. "Well, how can I choose to be Catholic if I don't know anything about other religions?" Dad thought about this for a moment, and then said he couldn't argue. I decided to wait until I knew more about other faiths and could consciously choose Catholicism. I have always taken vows very seriously. I would have felt guilty violating a single tenet and had to be sure. Later, my brother Tim wrote that this made me the most Catholic member of the family, since I took vows so seriously. I still do.

I mentioned that my father had one sister, Irene Carol. I never met her. Shortly after giving birth to her first and only child—Bill, conceived through marriage to her devoutly Catholic husband Frank Chauvin, an amputee veteran of World War II[5]—she was diagnosed with cancer. It had spread rather quickly to her ovaries, and the only known treatment at the time was radium and cobalt therapy. After consulting with the local bishop, Papa was told his only daughter could not be so treated; radiation would eliminate her ability to reproduce, and hence violate Church doctrine. While there is no assurance that the radiation and ultimate destruction of Irene's ovaries would have saved her life, this particular ruling had a profound effect on my father and, unsurprisingly, my sister Carol Irene:

> I grew up knowing my namesake died two weeks before I was born. I also grew up knowing our mother nearly died giving birth to her sixth son, my brother Mark. The Church refused to permit a hysterectomy and birth control. In my view, these were clearly not rational or compassionate stances of the Church, and completely inconsistent with Christ's treatment of women. My mother and aunt were treated as breeders, not human beings whose lives were at stake. Hypothetical lives were favored over actual ones. This never made sense to me, except as institutional misogyny.

Carol's ultimate decision to reject Catholicism and turn toward Eastern traditions like Buddhism took place years later, after the death of her closest friend John Rodgers, of AIDS.

> What exiled me from the Church with finality wasn't its treatment of women, but its criminal sheltering of pedophiles and simultaneous hatred of gays, including an often heartless stance towards AIDS.

These were institutionalized failings that went beyond human flaws. For me, they violated all sense of God.

To think of Carol as anti- or non-Catholic would be overly simplistic, however. "The truth is—I cannot unbecome Catholic any more than I can unbecome American," she writes. "It's not just cultural; it's cellular." To this day, she draws great sustenance from Catholic mystics and seeks occasional refuge in Catholic prayer.

> What speaks to me and for me is the writings of mystics across traditions—St. John of the Cross, Julian of Norwich, Teresa of Avila, Hildegard of Bingen, Loyola, Merton, Rumi, Hafiz, the Buddha.
>
> Still, as I kept vigil in those belly-of-the-night hours during Denny's agonized, final days [referring to our mother's death] all my acquired faiths failed me. I tried Sanskrit songs and Buddhist prayers, but none consoled, none even vibrated. Only Hail Marys reached the depth of peace I needed.

Not all Keeley children retain Carol's sense of the mystical and divine. "After a deeper than average, systemic investigation of major world religions," my brother Larry writes,

> I find most of them to be based upon nonsense. I have some affection for the God of Spinoza: broadly the notion that some "godlike presence" is embedded in the beauty, sophistication and systemic interdependence of all that we know due to

physics, chemistry, biology, etc. But I do not pray in any regular or organized way, and I do not attend any church services. I'm effectively an atheist. If I had to pick one world religion to force fit myself into, I'd say I'm a lazy Buddhist.[6]

This said, Larry does not entirely regret his religious heritage: "Perhaps thanks in some part to my upbringing as a Catholic, I continue to believe that it is imperative that I do good work in the world. In particular, I hold myself accountable for making a difference for the largest possible number of other human beings who are less fortunate."

Some never get to the point of raising questions about God, since they seem to experience no religious stirrings nor do they see why they should trouble themselves about religion.

Paul VI
Gaudium et Spes

In addition to Michael, my two younger brothers Ric and Mark are homosexuals. All three now characterize themselves as spiritual with an aversion to any religion that espouses unsympathetic views towards homosexuality, including Catholicism. It is not possible in full conscience to belong to an institution that labels one's innate and natural behavior "evil" or "intrinsically disordered." Indeed, homosexual inclinations and practices by thousands of priests show how profoundly difficult it is for anyone to defy their nature, even with solemn vows.

Man cannot live without love. He remains a being that is incomprehensible for himself, and his life is senseless, if love is not revealed to him, if he does not experience it and

make it his own, if he does not participate intimately in it.
John Paul II
Redemptor Hominis

Hypocrisy in sexual matters was one dividing factor for my brother Mark, but not the most damning. As a leader in the larger community of St. Louis, Missouri, responsible for respite care for thousands of special needs children and adults, Mark has been drawn into the struggles of the Armitage family. The Armitages hoped to have their son Christopher, who has Down Syndrome, enrolled in a local Catholic school. Despite their prolonged and patient efforts, however, local Church authorities have rebuffed the Armitages without satisfactory explanation. "The Catholic Church should institute systemic changes to include special needs children in parochial schools," Mark writes. "How can the Church exclude those individuals who Jesus reached out to the most?"[7]

Interestingly, both of my brothers' long-standing domestic partners—Rhey Castillo and Jay Fisk—describe themselves emphatically as Christians, though unaffiliated to any particular church or sect. Jay speaks passionately about his Baptist Church youth, with regular Sunday morning and evening services, Wednesday night services, Thursday night choir practice, baseball games, potlucks, and other youth group activities. Ultimately, though, his religious tradition by birthright rejected him:

> When my mother died after a lengthy illness, I was there in the bed with her, holding her, and talking to her about the joys of heaven and the peace she could finally have. She died in my arms and that was one of the most painful experiences of my life. It

was also the time I felt closest to God. I worried that I had not done it "right," so a couple days later I went to our minister and asked about this. He was dismissive, saying that he was sure that what I had done was fine. That Sunday his sermon was on the evils of homosexuality and how they (and therefore "I") were all going to hell. That was really my last day thinking I was part of any "church."

With three gay brothers and stories like this, it has been hard for many of us—including me, a practicing Catholic—to find Christ in the Church's teachings on homosexuality. The good news of the gospel is not intended for heterosexuals alone. Indeed, the infinite charity and mercy of God somehow seems foregone by many organized religions, especially when it comes to committed, faithful same-sex couples whose relationships often serve as models of fidelity and commitment.

> *The Church can see that certain customs not directly connected to the heart of the Gospel—even some that have deep historical roots—are no longer properly understood and appreciated.*
>
> Pope Francis
> Evangelli Gaudium

My sister Michelle married a Catholic and, like my brother Tim and me, raised her children with consistent exposure to Catholic traditions. Today, however, the Church's teachings seem out of touch to her:

I consider myself a Catholic who is distanced from the Church. While I believe it is a foundation for me I have grown disconnected as a result of some of its views and stances that are not current and relevant, including the role of women in the Catholic Church, birth control, and same-sex relations. I also believe some of its views are not consistent with the idea of an "all-loving Christ." In too many instances the Church has enacted doctrines of intolerance rather than acceptance. This has caused me to take "a step away from the Church"—figuratively and literally.

Among my brothers and sisters today, only Tim and I consider ourselves practicing Catholics. Interestingly, Tim's most important experience as a modern believer happened recently, while he lived in communist China 2009–2013. Through a group he met at his Catholic Church, he, his wife Veronique, and daughter Agatha taught English to poor migrant children just outside Shanghai. The program was so successful the Communist government shut it down. But for the Church, such outreach would not have happened. While none of his daughters consider themselves Catholic today, they too have been influenced by their religious upbringing; each has devoted their energies to social causes the Church lauds.[8]

I followed my brother Michael to the University of Notre Dame and—like my grandpapa, Hector—spent time at Moreau Seminary, seriously contemplating the priesthood. Desirous of my own children, however, I ultimately rejected the confines of a celibate life. Celibacy struck me (and still strikes me) as both unnatural and something I was unlikely to fulfill. I met my future wife —Saskia Bory, a Protestant from Geneva, Switzerland—while studying at Oxford. Because of my convictions, she agreed to raise our children Catholic. Her assent allowed us to be married in good standing with the Church.[9] I believe our variant views on God and the Church have been broadly beneficial to our children. Our two boys have so far taken the same path as their Aunt Carol: baptism and first communion, but not confirmation. It is clear both boys are still at early stages in their religious journeys. While Calum thinks of himself as Christian, Julian remains unsure. "I don't believe Jesus Christ 'died for our sins.' While the consistency between his words and actions strongly impresses me, moreover, I am not really convinced he was divine." Julian also vacillates in his beliefs about a loving Creator and the afterlife. Like many of their direct and distant cousins, neither Julian nor Calum dwell upon their own mortality or eschatological questions more generally. At this writing it remains unclear what their ultimate beliefs will be. We continue to engage on all these issues intensively.

Making sense of her mortality is what my cousin Debra Ludowe most appreciates about her Catholic heritage. "Understanding there is life after death—that is what I value most. In fact, it is the only way I can wrap my brain around death." Deb now characterizes herself as spiritual, however, and does not practice any religion formally. "I believe in God and I believe in Jesus. I believe Jesus rose from the dead and offers life everlasting. I do not believe God or Jesus judge us, however, and I don't believe in heaven or hell. I draw no guidance from the Pope, the Church and the Magisterium. I rarely go into a church, except on Good Friday."

Deb and her three sisters—Karen, Pamela, and Stefanie—had a wonderfully gentle, nonpracticing Jew as a father, George Ludowe. Like most Malette siblings, their mother Claire was a practicing Catholic. Today, none of the

Ludowe girls, their spouses or their children practice Catholicism.

> *Faith throws a new light on everything. It manifests God's design for man's total vocation, and directs the mind to solutions, which are fully human.*
>
> *Pope Paul VI*
> Gaudium et Spes

Juxtaposed against these doubts about organized religion and distance from the Catholic Church are the children of Uncle John and Aunt Mary, their ten grandchildren, and their chosen spouses. With few exceptions, all consider themselves practicing Catholics. "I have always been proud of my faiths and beliefs," Mary Kit Malette McGrath writes. "I accept most of the teachings of the Church, with the exception of birth control and the rights of homosexuals to share full lives with their chosen partners. I believe God wants everyone to be happy and treated equal." Weekly Mass, big celebrations around baptism, first communion, and confirmation, nightly Bible readings, signs of the cross on their foreheads, and a final prayer before being tucked in to sleep—the Malette-McGrath children were raised in a manner as traditionally Catholic as modern America knows.

Like Uncle John and Aunt Mary, Mary Kit and her siblings grew up attending Mass devotedly, and making frequent, special appeals to the Sisters of the Precious Blood, whose numbers included their great-aunt, Sister Mary Herman. Sister Mary Herman seems more than a lifelike figure in large part due to her constant joy, but also as something of a miracle worker. On more than one occasion, prayers to and with the Sisters of the Precious Blood were answered. For example, when Bill and Mary Kit McGrath's second child Erin was born, she had a number of red marks on her body and face, including her eyelid, nose, and upper lip. Mary Kit was alarmed, to the point of consulting a plastic surgeon. Aunt Rita (aka Sister Mary Herman) suggested that holy water be sprinkled on Erin's red marks, coupled with repeated prayer to the sisters for healing. By the time of Erin's second birthday, all the marks on Erin's face had faded. While those marks were unnoticeable, however, the marks on Erin's neck and back where Mary Kit did not apply the holy water are still visible to this day. "Glory be to God," Aunt Rita exclaimed.

Mary Kit's youngest sibling Michelle shares her mother's and sister's devotion to the Catholic Church. She has also done everything she can to pass her steadfast beliefs on to her children. "I most value having a shared faith and community where I belong and can worship. I go to Mass regularly to give thanks and praise, and to be nourished," Mich enthuses. "I believe Jesus is God made flesh, and that He is our redeemer and salvation. Only through Him are we saved from sin and promised eternal life with God, Mary, all the angels and saints and those who have gone before us." This said, Mich doesn't consider the Church faultless. "The human side of the Church is flawed, just like the rest of mankind," Mich states plainly. "But why do we always only focus on the bad things the Church has done? What about all the good that has been done—the charitable works, health care, education?" Mich also offers a more sinister interpretation of the Church's failings. She believes in the antichrist. "Has anyone ever thought that the Church is under attack by the devil? He tempts and weakens people, places doubt, jealousy, and selfishness. The devil's mission is to end all faith in God. He would only be too happy to see the Church fall."

> *I earnestly call upon pastors and the whole community of the faithful to help the divorced with solicitous care to make sure that they do not consider themselves separated from the Church.*
>
> *However, the Church reaffirms her practice, based upon sacred scripture, of not admitting to Eucharistic Communion divorced persons who have remarried.*
>
> John Paul II
Familiaris Consortio

The devotion of the John and Mary wing of the Malette family is all the more special as they have had to overcome another challenge: *divorce.* Uncle John left his wife Mary and their four children when they were young, ultimately devoting himself for life to another woman (who was also Catholic). Mary did not want this separation. Later, she attempted to have her marriage to John annulled, unsuccessfully. Given her special piety and devotion, this has been a source of unique pain for Mary. For her, holy communion has been disallowed. "I don't think the Church should withhold sacraments from faithful, divorced Catholics," Mary Kit writes, clearly feeling her mother's longing and pain.

Like her mother, Mich's marriage ended when her husband Martin Barry left her and their children when they were young. Again, it was not her desire, and in her conscience it was also not her fault. "I feel the journey of life is to love and forgive. My faith has helped me to do that, especially when things got rough. Now it is my responsibility to pass that same faith on to my children, so they can get through the tough times and be thankful for all they have." She has since remarried another Catholic, Mark Manders. Given how hard she tried to keep her first marriage intact, however, Mich emphatically believes she should not be denied communion. "God knows I did nothing wrong. Honestly, I feel He would be okay with me receiving Communion."

Mary Kit and Mich's brother, John, died tragically of a heart attack at the age of forty-five. He left behind a grieving widow Renee, three daughters, and one son, John Paul. As with Mich, however, their Catholic faith helped them through this difficult period rather than complicated it. "I am a practicing Catholic," Renee writes. "This said, John had far more faith than I do. I think it is because his mother Mary was so devout." At John's wake, Renee openly implored him for strength and courage, a vibrant display of her belief in life after death.

Two of John and Renee's daughters have since wed, Rachelle and Jacqueline. Their husbands, Kevin Christensen and Rob Biswas, have both converted (or are now in the process of converting) from Protestant faiths to Catholicism. John Paul just finished his second degree at Notre Dame, an MBA. Should there be any practicing Catholics in the next generation of Malettes, it would seem likely they would come from John and Mary's descendants. Sister Mary Herman would be particularly pleased, if so.

While John Sr. left his wife Mary for another woman, it would be wrong to characterize him as faithless or even un-Catholic. "There is nothing John would not do for someone in need," his sister Aunt Sue writes. "When he died, he had been reconciled with his Catholic faith for more than 25 years. He also helped bring my sister Claire back to the Church. In many ways, he was very much like Dad (Hector)." Among all of John and Mary's grandchildren, only two express some reservations about their Catholic heritage: Matt and Shannon McGrath. "We are both non-practicing Catholics," Shannon writes. "We both believe that being a good person is what really matters in life."

The last of the original seven Malette siblings with children or grandchildren who characterize themselves as practicing Catholics is Claude Malette. Claude's wife, Gloria, came from a long line of devout Polish Catholics, some of whom trace to the Third Order of St. Francis. Gloria's mother attended Mass daily. Their three sons—Chris, Paul, and Claude—all attended Catholic schools in various towns in Ottawa and Quebec, as their father's responsibilities at Chrysler dictated. Chris tells formative if harrowing tales of his time as a boarding student at Assumption Catholic College:

> Father Cullen and I locked horns from the start. The good father took me literally by the throat against a wall in his office in Grade 12, and told me "We're going to get one thing straight: I am the boss and you are not running your own show." Later that year Father Cullen made me manager of the vaunted Assumption hockey team—a squad that produced NHL caliber players with regularity. It was that move, I believe, that instilled in me a sense of honor, duty and responsibility that I carry to this day.

Apparently, not every corporal punishment meted out by men and women in the Church left permanent scars, though too many clearly have. Chris also divorced his first wife and has since remarried. This has not separated him from his Catholic upbringing and beliefs, however:

> I would characterize myself as a practicing Catholic, with caveats as I probably run afoul of some of the rules and regulations. I still hold many of the tenets of the Church true, while questioning some of the dogma. I place my strongest conviction in the last sentence of the Creed: "I believe in the Holy Spirit, the holy Catholic Church, the communion of saints, the forgiveness of sins, the resurrection of the body, and life everlasting."

Chris prays frequently "oddly, *through* my parents." Like virtually all Malettes and Keeleys, family is paramount to Chris and his two brothers, Paul and Claude. Still, Paul characterizes himself as an atheist, with strong affinity for the work of Christopher Hitchens and Richard Dawkins. Like his cousin Larry, Paul thinks much of religion is willfully ignorant of science and far too often the *source* of human conflict. Paul's wife Alicia and their children are spiritual and in the process of refining their belief systems. Youngest brother Claude— also divorced and remarried—designates himself as spiritual, too. His daughter from a first marriage—Brittany—is unique among the grandchildren of Claude senior and Gloria in characterizing herself as a practicing Roman Catholic. Her half-brother Ben and cousin Nicole instead think of themselves as Christian.

Final among the third generation of Malettes are the children of Madeleine Malette and Paul Thomson—Heather, Melissa, and David. While divorce again interrupted this union, Aunt Dee-dee (as we called Madeleine) remained close to her Catholic faith, even teaching for some time in parochial schools following her divorce. When knowledge of her second, common-law husband came to light, her employment was terminated. Madeleine eventually worked at an organization that helped battered women and children. She went on to specialize in child advocacy, with a focus on victims of abuse. In her last year of life she renewed her relationship with God and the Church—"coming full circle" according to her second daughter, Melissa. In the same year that Aunt Dee-dee died, Heather endured another, incalculable loss: her eldest son Matthew died of exposure after struggling for a period of time with substance abuse.

> What I value most about being raised Catholic is having faith in God, and the comfort of prayer my whole life, even if we did not go to church on a regular basis. The thing I regret is the guilt I felt.... I continue to pray daily, even though I have not attended Catholic services on a regular basis. Before losing Matthew I was a practicing Catholic. Now I feel I need a change. I have attended the local Alliance church a few times and have enjoyed how their service is not the same every week. I guess I would consider myself a non-practicing Catholic, but definitely a Christian, and still looking.

> *Our church doors should always be open, so that if someone, moved by the Spirit, comes there looking for God, he or she will not find a closed door.*
>
> *Pope Francis*
> Evangelii Gaudium

Siblings Melissa and David both think of themselves as spiritual. According to Melissa, "I believe there is a higher power/being but I also think that it is a manifestation of all people. I believe God is Love. I believe in reincarnation and that we are all here to learn. Love is the greatest achievement." Regarding how she and her husband—an ex-Catholic who now considers himself agnostic—will raise their children, Melissa writes, "Children need guidance but also the freedom to become who they are. This is a tough balance. Families share a common bond and should be able to rely on that bond when in need. Community also helps to raise children and protect them." Though some are still young, all of Heather, Melissa, and David's children consider themselves spiritual, still looking and open-minded to future revelations. Heather's daughter Breeanne seems to speak for many members of her generation who have been raised Catholic, peering into an uncertain future:

> I do think (and hope) that there is some sort of higher power than man and that there is some sort of life after death—I'm just not really sure what it is exactly. But I am content with this. I do not feel the need to "search" for the answer to what that higher power is as I do not feel there is any one "correct" answer. Everyone has their different beliefs. Nor do I feel searching will necessarily prevail any results. With that being said, I do not regret being brought up Catholic. I feel it has taught me good morals and provided me with a sense of faith as a child, which I needed in my younger years. However, as I have grown older, life experience coupled with gaining new knowledge has caused me to look at

specific types of faith differently. This has resulted in a change of my views on religion in general.

THE SYNOD'S TOP PRIORITY: GENERATIONS TO COME

Breeanne's honest depiction of her faith and the possible directions it may yet take provide helpful and urgent guidance for the General Synod that meets in Rome this fall. The decisions taken there as well as the tone of the messages sent will have profound implications for those who believe, those who don't and those who are still open to being led in new directions. As one of Breeanne's second cousins—Agatha Jane Keeley, youngest daughter of Tim and Veronique—told me, "Even though I am Catholic now, I cannot say what I will be in five years. Maybe I will still be Catholic, but maybe I will be something different. I just don't know."

Equally instructive, another member of the fourth generation—Marlia Keeley, youngest daughter of Larry and Beth Ylvisaker Keeley—speaks about how she plans to raise her own children:

> I would like to instill religious values in my children, including loving your neighbor and treating all individuals with respect, yet I do not know if I will raise my children with a specific religion. Instead, I would like to educate my children on all forms of religion and let them make a choice that is genuine to themselves. If they gravitate towards a

particular religion or set of beliefs, I will certainly support and encourage that interest.

But note Marlia's ambivalence and uncertainty about her own beliefs, something she appears to have inherited from her parents, and something that is sure to impact the lives of her children, and her children's children:

> I do not know whether a god or any other deity exists, yet I am hesitant to place such a strong label as "agnostic" on my views. I think that comes from a desire to want to believe in a higher power, or if not a higher power then some sort of existence which connects humanity and all beings on a deeper level. These viewpoints have evolved from my parents' religious views. My father, a "recovering Catholic" as he calls himself, has a VERY strong aversion to religion, particularly Catholicism. My mother, on the other hand, is extremely spiritual and has adopted all sorts of belief systems, ranging from Christianity, Buddhism, "spirituality," you name it. I believe this has made me very open-minded to different forms of religion, but also makes me uncertain of what is "right" or "wrong" or even real.

Marlia's sister, Brieze, grew up in this same household, and for years held similarly ambivalent views. While theirs was not an unspiritual home ("My mom always said grace before family meals beginning with the words, 'Heavenly Mother, heavenly Father'") Brieze's intense experiences in medical school forced her to look for stronger moorings:

As I had more exposures in the medical wards, I began to encounter a great deal more suffering. There is something unique about bearing witness to so many individuals making the transition from this life to the next, every day. The intensity of the experiences I shared with my patients made me want to carve out more intentional time each week to reflect on my faith and spirituality.

With this need for greater balance, Brieze found herself for the first time *ever* attending weekly religious services. She found out she actually looked forward to them, especially to being around other active Christians with shared, cherished values. She also met faithful people who lived their lives in ways she respected and admired. "I have found a church in New York that I absolutely *adore*," she writes. "It is called Hillsong. It is non-denominational, and each service seems more profound and inspiring than the last." Today she considers herself Christian:

My faith provides an anchor and a guiding light for me in times of great loneliness and uncertainty. As Pope Benedict XVI so beautifully said, "I have had moments of joy in life, but also moments when it felt like the Lord was sleeping." During joyful times, my faith enhances my rich sense of abundance, love and connectedness with my community and the world. It grounds me in values from which I choose consciously to live my life, even in the face of temptation or frustration. And it helps me continue to walk the path that I know is correct for me, every day. After all, as the Reverend Dr. Martin

Luther King Junior said, "Faith is taking the first step, even when you don't see the whole staircase."

But note importantly how faith has not *made* Brieze better or even good. Rather, it has helped her cope in times of stress, as well as sustain certain, desired types of behavior. My brother's partner Jay Fisk speaks of a similar "will to goodness" that manifests itself in believers and non-believers alike:

> I have worked with victims of domestic violence, homeless people, people with mental and physical disabilities, prostitutes, teen runaways, and many other "undervalued" people. I have met many, many people who do amazing work and face every day struggles with the spirit of God shining on their faces. Many of those workers have also left the Church and many have not, but I believe that all people doing the work of God are stewards of God, whether they consider themselves to be Christian or Jew, believer or atheist.

As I interviewed all my living relatives over many months and reflected upon the inspirational beliefs of my forebears, several convictions emerged. For one, I realized that the Catholic Church has a crucial role to play in providing guidance and hope, faith and joy to a very pained, still unjust, and overly angst-ridden world. I simultaneously realized the Church may fumble this opportunity. Without a convincing renewal, the Church could become more marginalized, increasingly shrill, alienating, and even a source of grave harm. Despite the energies and apparent desires of Pope Francis, I am sorry to say I find both outcomes equally likely.

In his treatise preparing the Synod for their portentous meetings this fall, Cardinal Walter Kasper wrote, "We are in crisis. The gospel of marriage and the family is no longer intelligible to many. For many it does not appear to be a livable option in their situation. What are we to do? Little is to be accomplished with good words alone."

Cardinal Kasper's concerns are well placed. Now, with the benefit of the Extraordinary Synod, it is clear Pope Francis is both encouraging and expecting an open dialogue as well as a renewal of the Church's deepest truths. All are to be congratulated for their efforts—both those who seek to defend traditions, and those who wish to broaden the Church's reach and relevance.

If bringing fallen and disheartened former Catholics back to the faith is important, and if the forgoing discussion of the real-life experiences of Keeleys and Malettes over four generations is indicative of challenges being experienced elsewhere around the world, it seems several clarifications and restatements of Church doctrine might help:

- *Allow divorced Catholics like Aunt Mary, Mich, and Chris, and other divorcees of proven goodwill to participate fully in the life of the Church, including the sacrament of Communion.* To most laypeople, it seems unfathomable that the General Synod will *not* endorse the policy of allowing longing, faithful, and truly repentant Catholics with limited responsibilities for their divorces the blessing of holy communion. Failing to do so would merely reaffirm a policy that appears to run contrary to the lengths and depths of the Lord's own mercy. Excluding faithful, remarried Catholics from the sacrament of communion would simultaneously convince thousands of wavering, yet-to-be decided spiritualists and budding Christians that the Roman Catholic Church is simply too rigid and unforgiving for their sensibilities.

- *Indoctrinate a more welcoming message and provide safe harbor to all homosexuals and same-sex couples of good will, like Mark and Jay, and Ric and Rhey.* The world was positively astounded when Pope Francis recently stated, "Who am I to judge?" speaking about homosexuals. The magnanimity of this remark should impress the Synod. Too many have become inured to the idea that judging is *all* the Catholic Church does. Not only would concrete actions to welcome practicing homosexuals like Mike back to the Catholic community result in the return of many gay men and women of faith; it would also impact their relatives—including nieces and nephews like Marlia and Brieze, Julian and Calum, and myself—to better believe the universality of the Church's message and relevance. True love cannot be evil, while hatred is always evil. The gospel must remain accessible to all men and women of good intention.

- *Provide for the real and whole needs of women.* Unlike Denise Keeley, Mary Kit consciously avoided having children before her life was threatened. Like most thoughtful women, Mary Kit knew best how many children she and her husband Bill could raise properly. My wife Saskia and I also elected to have two children only. The demands of modern life are simply too great for large families. As Carol stated, treating women as breeding machines is a form of institutionalized misogyny. It is also increasingly misguided in a world that desperately needs more female doctors, lawyers, teachers, leaders, AND mothers. A policy that effectively leaves loving parents exposed to bringing souls into the world they cannot properly care for is a form of tyranny. Birth control properly conceived could be completely consistent with a culture of life (including, importantly, the mother's) as well as part of a more comprehensive solution for remediating poverty.

• *Recognize that women—both lay and religious—have not been given roles and responsibilities in the Church commensurate with their skill sets and devotion.* There is a profound lesson to be learned from the dispute with the League of Catholic Women Religious (LCWR)—a dispute that has implicated both our beloved Adrian Dominican Sisters, as well as the order of Aunt Sue, the Sisters of the Holy Names of Jesus and Mary. That lesson is this: all women must be relied upon, heard, valued, respected, and honored. When they are, the world becomes more loving, just, balanced, and wise. The truly degrading treatment of the Adrian Dominican Sisters and other female religious led my eighty-six-year-old father Dick to doubt his Church and characterize himself as a nonpracticing Catholic.[10] It has also led my Aunt Sue to harbor unspeakable pain. To be wise, universal, and more God-like, the Church needs more feminine influences.

- *Practice genuine humility, and conduct genuine penance for past transgressions.* The Church has much work to do if she is to have any chance of reclaiming a meaningful measure of the moral authority she has lost in recent decades. The sins of pride, gluttony, sloth, lust, envy, wrath, and avarice are in evidence as much *within* the Church as *outside* it. The Church must lead by example. Not to do so gives license to cynics and the malevolent.

- *Don't attack the findings, virtues, and possibilities of science. Wherever they genuinely advance the human condition, laud them.* Paul VI writes in *Gaudium et Spes,* "The remedy which must be applied to atheism is to be sought in a proper presentation of the Church's teaching as well as in the integral life of the Church and her members." A fuller appreciation of the gaps that have repeatedly emerged between the frontiers of science and common Church doctrines would help those like Paul Malette and Larry Keeley regain respect for the faith into which they were born. The intricate mechanics and extraordinary promises of biology, physics, and chemistry are no less the Lord's creation than the miracles of Aunt Rita.

- *Finally, and above all—remember the children.* "If I could talk to the Pope," cousin Mich writes, "I would tell him that if the Church doesn't engage the youth more, we will lose all of them. They are our future. People are leaving the Church because they don't see what is in it for them. The Church must do more to remind our children about their ancestors' beliefs and why they are so essential."

How will future generations of Keeleys, Malettes, Ludowes, McGraths, Chauvins, Thomsons, Barrys, Biswas, Christensens, Borys, Flanagans, and other American families ultimately make sense of their lives? Will the Church provide them accessible, positive, inspirational, and actionable guidance—or will it alienate them with sterile, rigid, and incomprehensible doctrines and contradictory behavior? At this writing, in large part through the Extraordinary Synod, each of these questions have been asked. Too many remain unanswered.

By listening to the Holy Spirit and acting with pure love, the Church may yet divine God's will. As a parent with two intelligent, discerning, yet unconvinced sons, nothing for me could be more important.

2

THOUGHTS ABOUT REALITY AND SACRAMENTS

THOMAS KRAFFT

Reality is present in the space of confidence.
Klaus Ritter

⁓

Regarding the difficulties of the Catholic Church with the so-called *divorced and remarried*, I would like to highlight the concept of the reality that underlies a sacrament as such. As a philosopher, I don't see it as my task to criticize determined declarations of faith but to show the connotations and implications of said declarations. My point of departure is that the truth really exists. The reality of truth is demonstrated already in the fact that it stands out in our knowledge and marks the limits of our capacity to know. Knowledge never exists for itself; it exists only in relation with the truth. This relation with the truth we commonly call *faith*. The intent to found knowledge upon collective praxis, independently from any kind of faith, must be taken as failure, at least in the sense of a strong concept of knowledge. The failure of this intent corresponds to the transformation of the concept of transcendence, to which is related, in turn, our idea of reality. Whereas, for the believer, *transcendent* is that which surpasses our concepts, today it is considered *transcendent* that the individual consciousness ventures out beyond itself. With this I refer not only to the possibility of knowledge. The pragmatic possibilities of application must also presuppose the truth of their use along with faith. Today we learn to be impressed that we can understand each other and enter into communion one with another. At the same time we are aware of just how fragile and how exposed is precisely this community. The concept really set against faith is not, therefore, knowledge, but doubt.

It seems problematic that a philosopher would be occupied with a theological theme. The progressive process of specialization and differentiation in what we see and interpret tends in the other direction. Furthermore, behind the said process is the faith—or at least the confidence—that everything will turn out well. With this I do not intend to deny anyone the freedom not to believe. That is also possible. In this manner of seeing things, what we like to call *progress*, simply unstoppable, is nothing but a fleeing ahead or maybe the longing for something new, altogether distinct. Of course, these images also start from presuppositions; but given that it's a matter of completely negative presuppositions, I would like to draw precisely here the limit between faith and disbelief: faith accepts reality and presupposes, therefore, its goodness, while disbelief rejects reality as such. We must resist the dialectical-structural temptation to interpret this also as faith. Why? We must resist this temptation so that language may continue to convey meaning for everyone, thus maintaining the possibility of communion. The example of language allows us to make it clear that progress brings with it a danger that can be characterized as a fragmentation and parceling of reality. In this way the unity of the whole is lost. With this I don't mean to affirm, of course, that the whole falls apart, but only that it no longer represents for us the unitary context and horizon that we need in order to experience our life as meaningful. Decisive in all of this is the fact that this process is above all an illusion that only in a second moment becomes publicly effective. Thus, meanwhile it is supposed that in large measure God and man, spirit and matter, subject and object—to name only the most important of such pairs of terms—are clearly and unequivocally separated one from the other. Underlying this supposition is a determined idea of reality, which I wish to call *world*. Whereas reality is a happening, the world is a construct. Reality presupposes the existence of someone who carries out the work; the world, conversely, contains within itself, according to Immanuel Kant, the fundament of a universal interweaving. To the extent that this postulate must not be seen as more than a thesis contrary to God the Creator, it is not really a question of a position, but of a doubt in methodical form. Hence, the world is also always a suppression of that which we don't want to perceive.

THE SACRAMENT OF MARRIAGE AS A WORLDLY SIGN

The habitual theory of signs also starts from this conception of reality. According to this, we see every sign from two points of view. First, it refers to something that it itself is not. Thus, there is a traffic signal on which a red X on a dark blue background is enclosed by a red circumference. Every driver knows this sign and knows, consequently, that it prohibits parking the car in the place where the signal is found. The signal is the *signifying* aspect of the sign. But in addition to this there is a *significance* aspect, which in our example is that place which, with the help of the signal, must be kept or is kept free of cars. Hence we can understand a sign as an exhortation that is to be heeded, to the end that the sign as a whole be observed. On occasion, it happens that a driver decides to ignore a sign, whether he believes he can situate himself outside of the valid radius of the sign, or whether in so doing he obeys a second sign that he considers more urgent. I'd like to illustrate both possibilities. For the first case we can imagine a driver who happily parks his car wherever and, therefore, is confident that he won't be punished for his behavior contrary to the norms or doesn't care whether or not he is punished. The second case would be that of a driver who, having witnessed an accident, wishes to detain his vehicle without delay, get out, and give aid. If in these circumstances the space kept free thanks to the parking prohibition presents itself as a place to park, without doubt the driver acts correctly in conceding greater importance to the aid that must be given than to the traffic signal. In general it can be affirmed that signs, interpreted mundanely, are not effective alone, in virtue of themselves, but must always first be perceived, translated, and recognized. The effect depends secondarily on the sanctions that could be imposed in the case of not respecting determined signals. Such sanctions mark the difference between sign as offer (*An-Gebot*) and sign as prohibition (*Verbot*). In a sense, sanctions are necessary only when the signs are valued, even though not understood and universally recognized as containing meaning.

Many people understand sacramental marriage also as an action with the character of a sign. The woman and the man seal a lifelong alliance in a symbolic manner, making plain their intention to mutually support each other, bear conflicts together, and stay united whatever may happen. Following the previous example, we can consider this will of two people as the significance aspect of marriage, which in its turn is signified by other signs. According to this, to wear a wedding band signifies having a companion with whom one wants to be together. At any price? The sharing of life until the death of one of the spouses signified by marriage can only be presupposed as intention; whether or not such intention is also accomplished is another question. *Intention* always means wanting to exclude certain factors. At present, we interpret this rapidly saying that, in effect, until death do us part, unless…, as long as…; you never know what might happen. People separate, drift apart, and solicit divorce, as civil law allows. As a justification it is usually said that there was no longer anything in common, that one was deceived by the other, or even that living together was hell and that one is glad to have survived it. Note well: this is not a question of morality. Here it is not a matter of wanting to judge people or to classify personal destinies exteriorly.

Our effort pursues a secular or worldly comprehension of the sacrament of marriage. It is valued, sought, and celebrated because its possibility is understood as a romantic offer: party, solemn organ music, bridal gown, decorations, flowers, rings….For many, all of this expresses a longing for happiness and satisfaction—moreover, for eternal happiness and lasting satisfaction. Granted that in numerous cases this romantic aspect is also interpreted in a much more pragmatic manner, the imagined happiness at times shows itself to be volatile and the satisfaction to be relative. Perhaps the abyss grows between what one had imagined and still imagines and the day-to-day reality. Additional aggravations are conceivable, but they don't have to be listed here. What is decisive is that all too often the conclusion is drawn that it is better, whether for one of the spouses or for both, to follow anew each their own path. A horrible end is preferable to horror without end, affirms popular wisdom, with which is tacitly supposed, undoubtedly, the desperate nature of the situation. The spouses separate, which is easy for neither and also brings difficulties from the area of civil law. If we are permitted to overlook here exceptions of extreme aggravation, in the end the spouses usually come to the conclusion that they don't fit well together. It is taken for granted that each, considered separately, is a stupendous person, but only with much luck can another person be found who is also stupendous and additionally a good match. This is what we call *individualism*. But also as individuals we disassociate ourselves in body and spirit, problematic zones and points of controlled rupture, techniques of the *I* and possibilities of optimization. In light of the imagined, figured, and at times also experienced decomposition of everything, we fall back on ourselves, on our own *I* as the last reliable unit, which, however, most of the time doesn't suffice and cannot suffice of itself.

THE CHRISTIAN IMAGE OF MAN

Some might be surprised that this final point of numerous secular life projects corresponds precisely and exactly with the point of departure for the ecclesial interpretation of human existence. That the human being should turn his back on reality as a whole, enclosed in himself and his imagination, closed off to the other is, as *incurvatio in se ipsum* (curving over oneself, enclosing in oneself), what the Church classifies as sinfulness. On our own we cannot elude this curving of our *I*. Unfortunately, many people confuse sin and blame, so that they feel obliged to defend themselves against the interpretation of the Church. It cannot be insinuated precisely to the person who is alone and abandoned at the end of life, say some critical voices, that this person is to be blamed. Such an accusation against the Church amounts to a gross misunderstanding of what she wants to say. *Sinfulness* signifies that this is something that happens to everyone and that, therefore, we can't hide. That Adam tried to hide from God because of his fault would be comical if it were not already the expression of the sin of not wanting to live before God.

To speak of human sinfulness signifies, in the second place, that it is the human being himself who is exhorted to put an end to the intricate and unbearable situation. Herein is where the blame (*Schuld*) must be seen. But *blame* must not be understood here in the judicial sense, but rather in the sense of an obligation, as is suggested by the proximity of the German term *Schuld* to the English *should*. Our sin is, consequently, our loneliness; and our blame consists in the duty to seek the way out of loneliness. Our task is to become real in reality. This sounds somewhat cryptic or even esoteric; however, its meaning is self-evident. The fragmentary structure from which we compose our reality must be opened to all, such that, from this, it ceases to be mere opinion and figuration and we may begin to live together. I would like to illustrate this in reference to the three contrasting pairs mentioned earlier: God and man, spirit and matter, subject and object.

If as subjects we find ourselves before one or various objects or if we manage everything in a merely objective manner, this signifies, on the one hand, that we place ourselves in the center of the world—around which all the rest revolves—and, on the other, that at the same time we submit to the objects according to the type, the mode, and the extent of their availability. It would be better if we left off being subjects (subjugators and subjugated) and learned to open ourselves to what happens to us. The other is a question directed to us; we can be an answer. In this way, instead of thinking ourselves something and observing and measuring the other, we begin to find each other.

Spirit and matter are also interrelated. Either spirit is taken to precede matter, or it is affirmed that spirit arises from matter, or both are considered as coordinated without being able, however, to interpenetrate. The unity of both is not considered possible. Still and all, this unity is a condition for being able to confide in our perceptions, to get outside of ourselves, to approach and understand each other. In daily life we are aided by the idea that, really, only matter exists, but within the material mass there are also special bodies that contain a spirit. And since human beings are relatively similar from genetic point of view, it is supposed that also, in some way, the spirits in us function analogously. Thus understood, the links between people would be merely material. In this we can see the description of a real possibility, but not reality, for the perception of the body happens in the spirit and it is not possibly to reasonably distinguish between them. When I think of myself as matter, who thinks there, spirit or matter? And if it is the spirit that thinks, how can it think about itself if it is not with the help of the body? If we can manage, on the other hand, to understand spirit and matter as a unity, not only do we avoid undervaluing the body or viewing the spirit with reservations, but are also effectively enabled to confide in our perceptions and sensations.

The relation between God and the human being is likewise one of difference. It's true, of course, that not all that man thinks corresponds with God. However, sin does not consist in wanting to be like God, but in wanting to be like one imagines a god to be. God is not infinitely far from us; on the contrary. But we need a key in order to open our thought to the reality of God. This key is the cross. To comprehend this event in all of its extension, let us remember that which we have defined as the situation of man, as human existence. Man would like to be sufficient unto himself, understanding himself as his own lord and master. In this way, he loses sight of reality, which doesn't exist in parts, but only as a whole; otherwise it decomposes into fragments and aspects of perception. Then everything appears as random and relative. Whether or not it makes sense can be determined from this vantage point only a posteriori, that is, when it's already too late to intervene. What was taken as good at the time can later be classified as bad. The body and the spirit disassociate and rise up against each other. The finality of sin is the chaos of isolated individuals who struggle among themselves for survival.

Christ enters into this conceptual world in order to counteract such disassociation. The reality of Christ thus becomes the possibility of reconciliation and unity. Furthermore, the Church affirms that through the entrance of Christ, disassociation and disintegration have already been surmounted. Then, possibility would have been converted into reality. Hence, through Christ, God, whose Spirit acts in all and sustains all, is incorporated into reality. But, evidently, Christ does not carry out this healing ignoring the human being and apart from his will. Rather, he frees us to follow the way that was always there, but that only through him has become visible in an unequivocal and adequate light. He also called this way *the* truth and *the* life. But, why should we believe him? Why should we believe what he told us? On the other hand, is it perhaps more reasonable to believe that Christ is not the Son of God[1]? No; at least not while we are not offered at the same time something or someone as an alternative. Christ is for us the key to reality, and any other faith must be measured by the criterion of whether it helps—and if so, to what extent—to understand reality. *The* reality always implies the relationship between God and the human being, the reciprocal reference of spirit and matter, the unity of subject and object. To the extent that he bore the cross and let himself be nailed to it, Christ has shown us precisely in that same cross how we can enter into reality. The horizontal beam of the cross corresponds to being for others. Christ shows us that we can only be in harmony with ourselves, be one with ourselves, if we give ourselves to others. But to give ourselves to others signifies to confide in reality instead of wanting to affirm and impose ourselves, to fulfill ourselves. Perpendicular to this beam is raised the other, the vertical, as sign of our orientation toward God, who has become man. Blessed are the little ones and those who care for the little ones. Whereas all ideas of an adequate life favor a group of people more or less clearly delimited, thereby wronging the majority, the justice of Christ benefits all and applies to all. For if the small, weak, and poor are recognized as blessed, the evaluations are inverted at a stroke and the great, powerful, and rich are recognized as small, weak, and poor in reality. The limit of divine mercy is not justice, but the freedom of human beings to close off to love.

THE SACRAMENTS

In order to comprehend the position of the Church—and the difficulties that she encounters—on the question of the divorced and civilly remarried, we have to ask ourselves first of all what it is that must be understood by *sacrament*. We want to base the answer to this question on the *Catechism of the Catholic Church* of 1992, in which *sacrament* is interpreted from five different points of view. First, to the sacraments correspond deeds of Jesus Christ, partly as precursors of the sacramental actions and partly, however, as "'forces that spring' from the body of Christ (cf. Lk 5,17; 6,19; 8,46), always living and enlivening" (*Catechism of the Catholic Church* 1116). The Church acknowledges seven such deeds of Christ. Their repetitions are called *sacraments of the Church*, because they are administered by her and at the same time strengthen her. Second, the sacraments exist through and for the Church, but the Church does not exist through and for the sacraments, since the Church must be understood as directly instituted by Christ and, hence, as unrepeatable. The Church is the space in which the sacraments are effective. These are, third, at the service of the faith of the people, which they not only presuppose, but also "nourish, fortify and express by means of words and things" (*Sacrosanctum concilium* 59). The sacraments effect, fourth, the salvation of the faithful insofar as they are incorporated in the salvational event of Christ. This salvation is to be seen in that "the Spirit of adoption deifies (cf. 2 P 1,4) the faithful uniting them vitally to the only Son, the Savior" (*Catechism of the Catholic Church* 1129). With this, in the sacraments, fifth, the eternal life of the glory of God swells forth into terrestrial space and time, sanctifying them: "Worthily celebrated in faith, the sacraments confer the grace that they signify (cf. Council of Trent: DH 1605 and 1606). They are *effective* because in them Christ himself acts" (*Catechism of the Catholic Church* 1127).

These five points are closely related. While the last three characterize the *effect* of the sacraments, the first two determine the indispensable suppositions for the said effect to take place. The external condition is the Church, which in turn presupposes Christ, who is the internal condition of the sacraments. "They accomplish effectively the grace that they signify by virtue of the action of Christ and by the power of the Holy Spirit" (ibid., 1084; cf. also the following numbers). The sacraments are effective only because Christ has truly risen. Then, they take place in the space of the Church, which is the body of Christ. They operate, therefore, by incorporating the receiver of the sacrament to the action of Christ, thereby likening him to Christ. In the faith we become sisters and brothers of Christ. But at the same time our faith extends to the living work of Christ in us and through us, such that in him we believe also in the salvation that is communicated to us through him. This salvation is present in the sacraments, but not yet altogether. Thus, we could summarize the five points of view in the affirmation that *sacrament* essentially signifies the presence of Christ. This presence is experienced as grace undeservedly bestowed upon a person.

THE SACRAMENT OF MARRIAGE

"God himself is the author of matrimony" (*Gaudium et spes* 48). It's his reality, God's, that has it that a woman and a man find each other and unite, which determines the one for the other and keeps them together. This meeting is sanctified in the sacrament of marriage. "Following the fall, marriage helps to overcome withdrawal into oneself, selfishness, seeking one's own pleasure, and to open oneself to the other, to mutual aid, to the giving of oneself" (*Catechism of the Catholic Church* 1609). That's why it is not good that the human being be alone (cf. Gen 2:18). Now, the reason for this is simultaneously the reason that the union of woman and man is "threatened by discord, the spirit of dominance, infidelity, jealousy and conflicts that can lead to hate and rupture" (ibid., 1606). The woman and the man are made for one another, but in both the worldly *I* shows itself to be an autonomous power against their destiny. The freedom and well-being of the other are not always pursued, but often are assimilated to one's own ideas. Hence we must consider the community of the woman and the man weak and threatened in itself. It has consistency thanks only to the effort on both parts and to outside help. This help is always a grace of God, for it is he who guides us in reality. Confiding in his help it is possible for the spouses to remain faithful to each other even in periods of abysmal distancing.

"Following Christ, renouncing themselves, taking up their crosses (cf. Mt 8,34), the spouses can 'comprehend' (cf. Mt 19,11) the original significance of matrimony and live it with the help of Christ" (ibid., 1615). The woman and the man testify to this intention when they approach the altar together and, before the community, they administer reciprocally the sacrament of marriage. They put aside both their faintheartedness and their hardheadedness and ask God for help to fulfill the promise that they make, outsized from a merely human viewpoint, to remain together until separated by death. Since, "therefore, the bond of matrimony is established by God himself," it constitutes "an already irrevocable reality and originates an alliance guaranteed by God's fidelity" (ibid., 1640).

BREAKING A PROMISE

The intention of the bride and the groom to share life and to shape it together implies, from the Church's point of view, abstaining from all that could question this intention. Here is again manifest with all clarity the difference between the ecclesial and secular vision. Seen secularly, all intentions are subject to reservations; from the ecclesial perspective, conversely, trusting in the reality of God, the intention is sanctified and declared indissoluble. To retract such an intention equals, consequently, to retire confidence from God. Whereas judicially the *I do* of the couple is interpreted as a contract, for the Church it *is*, as a word mutually given, a nonabolishable reality—by not having the slightest arbitrariness—that is impossible to negotiate. In this sense, underlying matrimony is a decision (*Ent-Scheidung*, where *ent-* is a prefix that, in this case, indicates that something is reverted) by which is revoked the separation (*Scheidung*) of the human being into woman and man. The woman and man become *one* and will continue so until the death of one of them. It is not merely a question of the manner of fulfilling an act of language, but the realization of a destiny. It is always possible that spouses don't get along, but then they must see their task as bearing *that* and not act as if nothing had occurred. In the *Catechism of the Catholic Church* is stated that, with the existence of a valid marriage in the sense of the Church, a second marriage of either of the spouses, permitted by civil law, *objectively contradicts the law of God* (cf. ibid., 1650). This infraction constitutes, according to Jesus' own words (cf. Mark 10:11–12), adultery. But the second marriage differs from other faults in that, in it, the rupture of the first marriage, which is sacred, is prolonged and lastingly confirmed. Hence the divorced and remarried are also denied the sacrament of confession, unless they commit to "live in total continence." It is considered absurd to repent of an act only to later fall anew into the same error. But what must be understood by *total* continence?

I interpret this attribute as an allusion to Matthew 5:28, where Christ says, "But I say to you that everyone who looks at a woman with lust has already committed adultery with her in his heart." Compared to this dictate, the traditional imputation that the Church considers human sexuality as impure is shown to be wrong on all points. This imputation not only formulates a very simplistic criticism, but also demonstrates a lack of knowledge concerning the human situation. The sharp words of Christ refer us, conversely, to the heart as center of the person. The heart is where it really happens. In this sense, chastity is not an extrinsic category, but a means for protecting the human heart from distractions. To the protection of chastity corresponds, as counterpoint, the threat through sexual avidity, lust.[2] Avidity is not bad primarily because it exceeds all measure and creates discord, but because it devours the heart of him who, far from seeking and finding peace in himself from God, pursues it outside of his own existence and through the transformation of circumstances. The rest follows from here. Avidity clouds the view of reality through one's own conceptual world. The whole is interpreted as an accumulation of parts, which are perceived as disordered and that, consequently, must be ordered as considered adequate; only then will peace, satisfaction, and happiness be possible. If at first one still proposes to be truly happy under such and such circumstances, as lust grows, so grows personal dissatisfaction. But lust grows if it is not reined in by chastity.

Marriage is also a help in this sense for the person. Furthermore, it is a reality instituted and wished for by God. But, can we assume in all sincerity that the human being is able to perturb or threaten this reality? Doesn't the sacrament already signify that all is well? In Christ, the primordial sacrament (*Ur-Sakrament*), God has given his yes to all of creation.[3] As long as we want it, he accepts us just as we are and comes to meet us in the sacraments. Here it is not necessary to speak about our lack of justice toward him and his love. We are approaching, rather, the decisive point, namely, the impossibility of divorce. Why, from an ecclesial point of view, can't divorce be granted to a valid sacramental marriage? The Church bases her praxis on Matthew 19:6: "What God has joined together, let no one separate." This "man must not divide" is a translation from the Greek *me chroizéto*, that is, an imperative that must be understood in the sense of something that the human being is to avoid doing. Man *must* not elude God's destiny for him. Consequently, he *must* not revoke an alliance sealed by God. Whether or not he can do it is, however, a completely different question, a question with no room for a general answer, unless the human being wishes to put himself in God's place rather than follow him.

Here is where I see the decisive question: Can we interpret a mandate from the Lord as prohibition? Would not this imply holding God and his reality in low esteem? Does it correspond to us to impose sanctions? Wouldn't the renunciation of sanctions be precisely the expression of confidence in God's reality and the reality of the sacraments? Can our "hermeneutic principle to interpret truth," as Cardinal Walter Kasper writes, be anything other than divine mercy? Here we touch upon the difference between sacraments and secular worldly signs. Whereas these latter offer something that may, but doesn't have to be, observed, the sacrament occurs in reality. While, seen mundanely, free agency is realized in a reactive manner, that is, as reaction to a sign, regarding the sacrament freedom consists in opening and being able to open oneself to it. But by opening myself to the sacraments I open myself also to the other in his otherness, which is to say, also precisely there where he contradicts me. If this opening can be maintained, the marriage likewise turns out successfully. But the difficulty of human existence stems precisely from opening to the other. In Kasper's opinion, "For the sacrament to be effective…it is indispensable to believe in the living God as goal and happiness of mankind, and in his providence, which desires to guide us on our way towards the definitive goal and happiness."[5] Does this mean that the sacraments are real only if they are believed in and while they are believed in? Most likely not. Precisely as an offered position, we must understand the sacraments as irrevocable realities. Divorce always signifies a heavy mortgage, which weighs upon a second attempt. In this sense, in no way *can* the human being divide that which God has united.

Still and all, Gilbert Keith Chesterton exaggerates by making an absolute of the ontological component and thereby characterizing the possibility of divorce as superstition.[6] In this respect Kasper writes, "The good news of Jesus is that the close alliance between the spouses is embraced and backed by the alliance of God, which continues to exist thanks to God's fidelity even when the fragile human bond of love weakens or is even extinguished."[7] The fidelity of God guarantees the alliance, but doesn't coincide with it. God remains faithful to us, though we are unfaithful to him, unfaithful to each other, and even to ourselves. This fidelity sustains us even when we make mistakes, as long as we confide only in God and, therefore, want to spontaneously avoid errors. This is also valid when we find ourselves forced to break our word given to the other or, better put, to go back on it. For Kant, the possibility to make promises is what distinguishes us from animals; and also for Kasper, "It is proper to human dignity to be able to make definitive decisions."[8] From there it doesn't follow, however, that whoever breaks a promise degenerates into an animal or loses his dignity, and from then on can be treated differently than other people. Rather on the contrary: precisely because he runs the risk of doubting himself and falling into desperation, whoever cannot keep a promise needs support. If he asks for forgiveness, it is our duty and task to forgive him. According to the philosopher Robert Spaceman, to forgive even constitutes the true dignity of the human being: "To forgive is an eminently creative act." To forgive enables the person to promise anew, to dare to make a new promise.[9] With this it is also probable that, as Chesterton feared, the new word is in turn a rupture of the old.

THE PARABLE OF THE TALENTS

In the question raised by the divorced and civilly remarried it must be supposed that for them it is something serious. We can start from the person for whom exclusion from the sacrament of communion is a problem that causes suffering. Can't we, even today, presume in general that everyone who solicits a sacrament (with the exception of the sacrament of marriage, socially fashionable), is already prepared to receive the sacrament by this alone? Isn't that also reality? The social pressure that for a long time induced many people to desire sacraments without the necessary disposition has been inverted to just the opposite sense. At present certainly no one runs the risk of *giving away* the sacrament if he invites to participate in it.[10] This, of course, does not exempt the Church from her obligation to remind those who want to participate in the holy communion that that which they solicit and receive "is the body of the Lord" (cf. 1 Cor 11:27–29). But she can't do more. It is not the Church's competency to decide about the dignity of a concrete individual. In a certain sense it can be affirmed that no one is worthy to receive the body of the Lord, for he has given himself to us by pure grace. Hence we pronounce the words of the pagan centurion before receiving the holy communion.

What remains open is then the question of the awareness of—or the opening to—the sacrament. But here also it's true that the Church exists to distribute, not to impede. The cheat, more than taking in the Church, takes in himself. Possibly, the parable of the talents that Jesus relates (cf. Matt 25:14–30) deals not only with each individual, but also with the Church. Among the talents, are not the sacraments the greatest? Aren't these the condition for the talent to give fruit? Are they not themselves at once talent and fruit? In them, Christ has confided his fortune to the Church. Thus, when a person approaches the Church and asks to be conceded forgiveness and the grace of the Lord, can she think of denying them?

Wouldn't she then be like the third servant of the parable, who for fear of God wrongly interprets the parable, in which God reaps where he has not sown and gathers where he hasn't scattered? But the sacraments are not just seed and straw as are other signs, but in themselves are already fruit. In them our searching yes is answered. It seems so to me as a philosopher. It's possible that I've overlooked something that theology wishes to and should take into account.

CONCLUDING CONSIDERATIONS

With this we now find ourselves also facing a fundamental difficulty for understanding the ecclesial conception of sacrament. In a sacrament only God operates. Hence the sacrament accomplishes precisely that which it signifies. In consequence, we can't understand what a sacrament is without participating with faith in its realization. Nor do we know what happens when someone "receives" a sacrament, accepting it without faith. We don't know if something happens or if the problem must now be seen in that the receiver only acts as if he received it, that is, he receives it *un-really*. In one respect, he can think that he knows what a sacrament *is* (which is to say, that it's *nothing*), but on the other hand, between the reality, which is the meaning of all, and himself he has introduced his own idea that obstructs his vision. The truth defends itself. Whoever positions himself against it already has sufficient punishment in living in the absence of truth, in thinking he knows reality when he doesn't, in believing that there is nothing worth searching for.

To whoever experiences it in reality, the presence of Christ is given completely as sacrament. But it is only given to those open to it and missed by those moved by doubt. If we open ourselves, we forget ourselves, whereas, if we represent a world to ourselves, we forget both the others and the other. Hence the difficulties of the Catholic Church with the divorced and remarried are not a matter of signs or of interpretation; moreover, it would be wrong to interpret the non-admission of the sacraments as punishment for a previous infraction. This is evident for anyone who takes seriously the triumph of Christ's impotence over the worldly power of death. Consequently, it is possible to attribute the difficulties of the Church in dealing with the divorced and remarried to the fact that it is the Church's task to demonstrate the great in the small.

When the Church warns of the risk of not recognizing the seriousness of the sacraments, it does not denote a hidden unmerciful avenger, which could only seem a threat even to the most devout; rather, it's just the contrary. God accepts us such as we are. To the extent that she takes the sacraments for sacred, the Church accentuates their effectiveness. To the extent that she keeps them at a distance, she indicates the *sole* condition for the sacramental event becoming real: it must be beseeched in prayer. The sacraments are expression of Christ's already achieved victory. Like a door, they are open to everyone to pass from the darkness of worldly suffering to the splendor of the glory of Christ. This mercy wants to be perceived. It is an event through which and in which we are enabled to shake off our finite dependencies and attachments, to the end of being free for the reality of Christ, who sustains and penetrates all.

3

CHILDREN OF GOD IN THE FAMILY OF GOD

Models and Impulses of the New Testament

THOMAS SÖDING

GOOD BEGINNINGS: CONJUGAL LOVE AND DIVINE LOVE

In the social environment the slogan *bad news is good news* is current. Marriage and family are no exception in this respect. Marital scandals appear to be more interesting than marital happiness. The divorces of prominent couples are appetizing; lasting relationships are hardly mentioned. When a family has split, enormous attention is incited, be the sentiment fake or authentic; when a happy family is spoken of, envy and suspicion is the order of the day.

In the current debate of the Catholic Church, it's necessary to be all eyes and ears so that this same slogan doesn't subtly creep in. Doubtlessly, there have to be good solutions, theologically founded, for those whose marriage fails—above all, for the children, the ones who most suffer with the separation of the parents, but also for the couples themselves: in the first place, for the "cheated," though also for the principally guilty. When in marriages and families there is violence and abuse, deceit and betrayal, a way of reconciliation that opens to the future is necessary.

In these important discussions it is not right to forget those whose marriages are maintained or those who wish to promise themselves in matrimony. These are, by far, the most numerous, thank God. To be sure: when heaven resounds with violins, the refrain, "He who ties forever, tie loosely!" is appropriate. However, "Yes, we can" is also valid. And for those who have spent many years together and perhaps know the joy of having children, not only "A rolling stone gathers no moss," but also the other refrain, "Time heals all wounds," pertain. In light of these pairs of refrains, the slogan should run, "Good news is good news."

But it is not enough just to better divulge this good news. It is necessary to relate it to the *only* good news that merits faith: the good news that Jesus announced. This is the great opportunity offered by the Catholic doctrine of the sacramentality of matrimony. No human being can attain to the infinitely great love of God for mankind. But in the mutual *I do* spoken by a man and a woman a spark of this love can flash forth: in *éros* saturated with *agápe*.

GOOD EXAMPLES: SYMBOLS AND STORIES

In the New Testament are found the encouraging images of the banquet of the celestial wedding, which figure already in the Old Testament. It is the portrait of the Messiah, as husband, who celebrates his wedding with Israel, as wife, the daughter of Zion; it is the category of the alliance that God seals with his people and to which he is faithful even when men become unfaithful; it is the poetry of the ode to love (1 Cor 13), appreciated by many engaged couples because in the ode to God's love, enkindled in the human heart, they discover their own love that they wish to share throughout life; and not least, it is the doctrine of Jesus on marriage, the union of man and woman, both created in God's image in order to mutually recognize one another. Jesus himself lived celibately—for the kingdom of heaven! His celibacy does not demonstrate, however, any contempt or fear of matrimony; Jesus shows, rather, how marriage can be a "sacrament," a "mystery" of God's encounter with human beings through God's love, which draws infinitely near to men.

Of course, in the New Testament and in biblical science other pages are read: that Jesus represented an "a-familiar *ethos*"; that his motto is "to abandon"; his watchword is conversion and beginning anew, not "go ahead." Isn't there the irritating tradition that Jesus said, "For I have come to set a man against his father, and a daughter against her mother, and a daughter-in-law against her mother-in-law"? (Matt 10:35; cf. Luke 12:53).

In effect, that family ties are sacrosanct is a Roman and Jewish idea more than of Jesus. In case of conflict, in Jesus and the apostles the voice of conscience and the call of faith always prevail. This principle penetrates even Catholic matrimonial law, which, resting on Paul, permits divorce and a new marriage if otherwise faith would suffer detriment. There can be no tie that impedes the advance of faith, not even those with other family members.

But from the priority of faith destruction does not follow; rather renewal of the marriage and of the family does.

Precisely in the gospel is seen clearly how good both are: they are a yes to the God of life, who makes the promise of eternal happiness, not because for him earthly happiness means nothing, but because this happiness can increase only when people are able to hope for it in their most audacious dreams.

In this perspective, the New Testament recognizes many good marital narratives. They're not as fully developed as the Old Testament account of Abraham and Sarah or the love stories of Ruth and Tobit. It's a matter of precious miniatures. They don't pretend to woo an archangelic world, but they do allow seeing into the force of faith for uniting the love of God and neighbor in this completely special form of conjugal love.

GOOD HOPE: ELIZABETH AND ZECHARIAH

Luke begins his Gospel describing the world from which Jesus comes. It is the world of pious Jews—men and women—who observe the law, who wait for the Messiah, who venerate the temple. They are the silent ones of the country. But they are those to whom matters the love of God above all else. For this reason, they are the poor, who have a sixth sense for the love of God and who most need his blessing, but also those who most feel it.

However, they are not people without problems and doubts, questions and fears. Elizabeth and Zechariah are the best example. As presented by Luke, they are exemplary in their piety and righteousness, in their sensitivity and inspirations. They are profoundly rooted in Jewish life, by family and by profession; Zechariah works as a priest in the temple of Jerusalem. But they have a serious problem: they have no children. In antiquity, when there was no good information about feminine health nor maternity care or social security, the problem was even greater than for modern families without children who desire them with all their heart. This was especially hard for the women. When in doubt, the blame was laid on them. In Luke it is possible to recognize this judgment that is conditioned by its time. Outright, it is said that Elizabeth was "barren" (Luke 1:17). So the suspicions of the people are cast on her. *Barren* signifies public shame, even punishment for some hidden fault that must be expiated. When everything had changed, Elizabeth exclaimed: "This is what the Lord has done for me when he looked favorably on me and took away the disgrace I have endured among my people" (Luke 1:25). The humiliation is the social scorn that is augmented by religious motivations; in a traditional society as at that time, for which the contrast of honor and humiliation have supreme importance, and in a family to whom above all matters God's love, this confession of faith can have come only from a profoundly wounded heart that had been healed.

Against all custom, the boy is to be called *John*, which means "God is merciful." With this boy, the long, childless years that Elizabeth and Zechariah have borne faithfully together are not left devalued. On the contrary, neither is John going to found a family, but he put himself entirely at the service of the Messiah who was to come. It is not a matter, then, of the right to reproduce, which, nevertheless, in the last instance, is fulfilled. It is, rather, that the lack of children is not considered as public shame or punishment and that the happiness of a family is not dependent upon the blessing of children. Moreover, like John, each child is the result not of human generative vigor, but a gift from God to which, as father and mother, nobody has a right, but can only receive, protect, educate, let go...and always, love.

GOOD NEWS: MARY AND JOSEPH

Completely distinct from that of Elizabeth and Zechariah is the family situation in the case of Mary and Joseph. Luke narrates the story from the perspective of Mary: how faith grows from awe and questioning; how careful looking leads to reflection and comprehension. Matthew recounts the story from the perspective of Joseph: it's clear that, without the message from the mouth of an angel, he can't believe what has happened. Patrick Roth, in his novel *Sunrise. Das Buch Joseph*, has described the tremendous tension that marked Joseph throughout his life. The novel goes beyond the Bible. But in it Joseph's righteousness, which can only come from faith, is translated from Matthew to novel with extreme density.

From the angel who appears to him in dreams Joseph receives two great charges: he must receive Mary as his wife, and to the child that she is going to bring into the world he must give the name *Jesus* (translated: "God helps"). Both charges are established by the angel. Joseph must not turn Mary away, "for the child conceived in her is from the Holy Spirit" (Matt 1:20); he must give Jesus his name "for he will save his people from their sins" (1:21). Joseph does exactly what the angel has charged him: "He took her as his wife" (1:24), and the child, whom he took as his own, "He named him Jesus" (1:25).

Whoever continues reading Matthew's account of the infancy recognizes with what foresight and energy, what solicitude and capacity for action Joseph takes on his role as father: he saves Jesus' life, defending him from the attack of Herod, the infanticide; he organizes the escape of the family to Egypt and their return to Nazareth. Christian art takes pleasure in the images of the "Holy Family," which, in the best examples represent, not the quaintness of an idyllic family, but the drama of a family of emigrants.

The paternity of Joseph, in Matthew, is not defined biologically, but ethically and theologically: Joseph can fully serve as a model for all of those parents who care for the children of another couple or adopt. Paternal love is not chained to the genes; in true love and true hope, it can move beyond the borders of biology.

Following the narration of the infancy, Joseph recedes in the Gospels to the background. "Is not this the carpenter's son?" ask the inhabitants of Nazareth when Jesus appears with signs and miracles, words and deeds (Matt 13:55)—and they have no idea how to deal with the skepticism they express. To know Jesus as the Messiah is difficult for them because they think they already know him, and yet, they contemplate him only superficially.

What about Mary? According to the Gospel of Luke, she is a very peculiar mother marked more and more by the good news she has heard and by the faith this good news has given her. In no passage of the Gospel is it given to understand that the mystery of Jesus was clear to Mary from the beginning. Mary is, rather, a young maiden who has questions and seeks answers. She "makes haste to the mountain" to aid her relative Elizabeth. She is characterized as prayerful psalmist and inspired poetess, able, in the Magnificat, to find the adequate words for uniting the salvational action of God with her people, to the advantage of all peoples by the grace that she has experienced. She is a worshiper who can unite gratitude with excited expectation, love of God with love of mother. She is a mother who gives birth to her son not in a lovely home, but in a stable. And, not least, she is a mother whose son has so touched her heart that her love becomes, rather than blind, clairvoyant.

Three key scenes stand out. At the end of the nativity story it is said, "But Mary treasured all these words and pondered them in her heart" (Luke 2:19). Taken literally, the second part of the phrase reads, "she composed it" or "she assembled it" because she was attentive and could remember. She was able to discover the relation between the road to Bethlehem and the birth of Jesus, between the newborn in swaddling clothes in the manger and the shepherds' visit, between the glory of God and peace on Earth.

At the end of all the narratives of the infancy it is said: "His mother treasured all of these things in her heart" (Luke 2:51). In the jewelry box of her heart was now also kept Jesus' question to her, she who had been anxiously searching for him when, on the journey to Jerusalem, Jesus acted on his own: she—the same as Joseph—couldn't have known to which world he belonged and where he could be found, if not there where God's wisdom is seated: in the temple, the goal of their pilgrimage.

In between are the circumcision and the presentation of Jesus in the temple. Mary is accompanied by Joseph. But the prophecy of the elder Simeon refers only to her: "A sword will pierce your own soul too" (Luke 2:35). The *Mater dolorosa* has always touched hearts. Mary is a mother who has lost her son—and by this means has recovered him, forever. Luke presents her as model of faith as well as consolation for all mothers and fathers who have lost a child: because there is Jesus, the son of Mary, who has died and come back to life, death does not have the last word, for love is stronger than death. Christian art has represented the grieving mother in the Pietà, at the foot of the cross, with the dead son across her lap. But in the Gospel of Luke, this participation in the passion already begins before; and the capacity for reflection, the intelligence and the life of the heart of Mary are based exactly on this: in that she, as a mother, takes part in the life of her Son, whom she bore in her womb and brought into the world.

GOOD COMPANY:
THE APOSTLES AND THEIR SPOUSES

Paul wasn't married. He lived and valued celibacy (1 Cor 7). But, in this aspect, he is the exception rather than the rule. This can be deduced, at least, from a small "self-defense" in which he relates the freedom of his apostolic ministry, that incredible "to be all things to all people," his right to dispense with rights, especially the sustenance owed to him by the communities of mission. To expressively describe this renouncement of rights, Paul writes, "Do we not have the right to our food and drink?" (1 Cor 9:4). It is understood "at your expense." He continues, "Do we not have the right to be accompanied by a believing wife, as do the other apostles and the brothers of the Lord and Cephas?" (1 Cor 9:5). Paul argues in such a way that this praxis appears evident to the Corinthians. The apostles were married before their call. The following of Jesus doesn't unleash a wave of divorces, but transforms the life of the married. The present and the future of both spouses fall under the sign of the mission. The expression must be understood well: in mind are not housewives but spouses, and that these, in the meantime, have equally opened to the faith in Christ, remain faithful to their husbands, and accompany them on their missionary trips. Much is said about the profound changes in the life of the apostles, and especially about Peter (Cephas): the fisherman who became a fisher of men and, therefore, itinerant missionary, and, consequently, martyr in Rome. But almost no one ponders the other aspect: that for the women it was no small challenge to leave house and home to find new houses in new countries, with other languages, other lifestyles, other cultures...and much less is said about what this meant for the marriages and families: how stable and vital, how firm and adaptable they must have been in order to stand the pressure of change, but also to assure the vital base for the missionary activities.

Descriptions are lacking of the daily life of the missionary couples. But at the beginning of the Gospel of Mark there is a small scene that reflects it. It takes place in the "house of Simon and Andrew"; James and John are present. It is recounted because it preserves a historical memory important for its exemplarity. The central point is the cure. But it is important how this is realized: "The mother-in-law of Simon was in bed with a fever, and they made it known to him right away. He approached her..." The situation adjusts perfectly to the image of that time: the sick woman is in bed, a bit apart. But Simon and his brother Andrew are concerned about her, and inform Jesus. Jesus helps: and, in this way the family is newly reunited. Not many words are needed to measure the importance: Jesus cures so that things may go well for the apostle's family. This is a sign.

GOOD CONTACTS: TIMOTHY AND HIS FAMILY

Paul was no "lone wolf," but a *team player* (of course, as the captain). One of his most important collaborators is Timothy. He came from Lystra, in Asia Minor; he is the son of a Jewess who had become Christian and a Greek who probably remained faithful to his old gods. Having a Jewish mother, Paul treats him as a Jew who has attained to faith in Christ and, for this reason, circumcises him correspondingly—not because circumcision was in any way necessary for the faith, but out of respect for the Jews, as Luke writes (Acts 16:1–5). As collaborator of Paul, Timothy took on numerous responsibilities and continuously carried out delicate missions—among others, in Thessalonica (Acts 17:14ff; 18:5; 1 Thess 3:1—5:6), in Macedonia (Acts 19:22) and in Corinth (1 Cor 4:17; 16;17; 2 Cor 1:19).

In the Second Letter to Timothy he sends an authentic literary piece. In early times, this letter was dated at the end of Paul's life; today it is attributed generally to a Pauline school and is dated at the end of the epoch of the New Testament canon. Paul confesses that he misses Timothy—like a father misses his son—whom he hasn't seen for a long time (2 Tim 1:4), and goes on, "I am reminded of your sincere faith, a faith that lived first in your grandmother Lois and your mother Eunice and now, I am sure, lives in you" (2 Tim 1:5). Immediately after, Paul speaks of the grace that has been deposited in him by the laying on of hands and that it must be newly inflamed (2 Tim 1:6). It is, then, also a decisive text for the history and the theology of the Church.

So much the more important is it, then, that the family roots are not forgotten, which for Timothy are as important now as they were before. His faith is rooted in his family; he learned it there and there took it on—that faith that sustains him until today, says his mentor Paul. There are two essential aspects. One: there are two women whose names are cited. It can be lamented, but thus it was from time immemorial and thus it continues more or less today: that it is, above all, the women who look after the education of the children and, therefore, are the most important witnesses and teachers of the faith. The second aspect: the mother and the grandmother are Jewish. This can be interpreted in two ways: that either there has been a conversion of generations en bloc to Christianity, and it is this conversion that Paul remembers, because Timothy benefits from it now as then; or, Paul thinks that it was the Judaism of his grandmother, as well as his mother's, that has marked Timothy and whose imprint he must continue to receive. In favor of this latter thesis is the fact that Paul, in the previous phrase (2 Tim 1:3), roots his Christian faith in the faith of his Jewish ancestors. If it is to be interpreted in this way, the family is indicated as the ambience of faith that permits a profound renewal, without betrayal of the past and while belonging to the family.

GOOD RELATIONS:
PRISCA (PRISCILLA) AND AQUILA

Paul was often unjustly accused of misogyny and as an enemy of the family. It's true that he himself lived celibately.

But almost no one has done more for women and families. The decisive point is that he advocated baptism, which is the same for men and women, whereas circumcision, the seal of belonging to Judaism, was performed only upon males (thanks to God).

Especially picturesque is the portrait drawn in the Acts of the Apostles. In his account of the activity of Paul in Corinth, Luke notes, "There he found a Jew named Aquila, a native of Pontus, who had recently come from Italy with his wife Priscilla, because Claudius had ordered all Jews to leave Rome. Paul[a] went to see them, and, because he was of the same trade, he stayed with them, and they worked together— by trade they were tentmakers" (Acts 18:2–3). From professional colleagues, they convert into friends; from emigrants, into allies; from companions of faith, into companions of mission. Aquila and Priscilla are married and Christian; because of their Judeo-Christian faith they have been exiled from Rome; in Corinth, a new Roman colony in Greece, they have settled anew and opened to the public an artisanal business; they show Paul hospitality; they offer him salary and sustenance. But one thing stands out: how great had to be the harmony, the capacity for work, the talent for organization; how great had to be, above all, the faith of this married couple to overcome exile, undertake a new beginning, and yet still maintain an open house, open hands, and an open heart!

But the story gets even better. Because later, Luke relates, Paul puts to sea with the two of them headed for Ephesus, the capital of the Roman province of Asia, not far from Pontus (all in modern Turkey). There they settle in (Acts 18:18–19) and form a missionary team. Luke recounts that they won over to the faith none less than the famous wise maestro of Egyptian Alexandria, Apollo, who had known only the baptism of John, and initiated him in Christianity. "When Priscilla and Aquila heard him, they took him aside and explained the Way of God to him more accurately" (Acts 18:26). They are a catechism team. As with Paul, they practice hospitality. It's evident that they don't shrink before his prestigious eloquence. They seek Apollo precisely there where he is: in the baptism of John and in all of the promises gathered in it. It's clear that they form a good team, not only professionally but also in the faith. They don't play the same role as their friend Paul. But without people, without married couples like these, the faith would not have been transmitted (within families, but also outside of them).

In his letters, Paul also mentions Prisca (as he calls her) and Aquila. From Ephesus he sends to Corinth greetings from them, and adds: "together with the church in their house" (1 Cor 16:19). The Apostle links together the old acquaintances; it's clear that neither has left Corinth due to any conflict, but that they maintain good contacts—which Paul can now recall and through which he can establish relations. In addition to this, they, as a family, but beyond their relationship as a couple, have formed one of the small Christian cells whose vitality has been very great. Conjugal selfishness...banish the thought! Prisca (Priscilla) and Aquila are one of those Christian marriages without which the Church could in no way have kept afloat throughout the years until today. Children are not mentioned. Perhaps they are implicit in "the house." But, regardless of this, the couple irradiates a missionary fervor that, from their house, reaches the city, and from Ephesus reaches Corinth. Paul himself seems fascinated by it.

From Corinth he again sends greetings to both in Rome: "Greet Prisca and Aquila, who work with me in Christ Jesus, and who risked their necks for my life, to whom not only I give thanks, but also all the churches of the Gentiles. Greet also the church in their house" (Rom 16:3–5). It is to be supposed that they, like many others, had been able to return to Rome. It's clear that, as in Ephesus, they have formed a known and recognized community. But, more than all of this, Paul has most high praise for their commitment to the Church: he calls them his "collaborators," because they have also played an active role in the mission and in the catechism, for the construction of the Church and the growth of the faith. He praises their generosity on his behalf, with which perhaps he is thinking not only of their support when he first set foot in Corinth and their help in opening a missionary path. This generosity refers not only to him: no sooner had Prisca and Aquila begun to move in the wings than they achieved a high degree of notoriety (and it seems clear that they are loved and appreciated by all).

They haven't played this active role as itinerant missionaries, like Paul. In spite of their mobility, it's clear that they always maintained a special local presence. Expelled from Rome, they take the first opportunity to return there. In Corinth, Ephesus and Rome they practice Christian hospitality, opening their doors and taking in people who, for their part, are also on the move, so that in crossing the desert they find an oasis whose water doesn't stagnate, but always flows fresh. Without family unity, this would be unattainable; and without family inspiration by the spirit of the gospel, impossible.

GOOD HOUSES:
LOVELY MANSIONS AND OPEN DOORS

This way of life of Prisca and Aquila is the recipe for the success of the Christian mission as developed, above all, by the Apostle Paul. He himself remains relatively little time in one place: a week or two, or a month or two; only by force of necessity and as an exception, somewhat longer. He has understood his personal mission as announcing Christ there where no one has yet heard speak of him. But this formula changes when the sown seed has fallen onto fertile soil, so as to take root, grow, and give fruit.

The most important field to be sown was the "house." This is seen as clearly in the Acts of the Apostles as in the letters. Just an example: the first European Christian of whom the New Testament informs us is Lydia, a tradeswoman from Philippi whom Paul meets at a Jewish prayer site before the gates of the city; once convinced of the faith, she invites him to come to her house, to form part of the family, and to continue his activities from there (Acts 16:11–15). We are not told about all who form her household, or if she had a husband and children. But the "house," in antiquity, is not just a building, but a form and a community of life, whose center is the family.

From archaeological and historical investigations quite a lot can be known about the houses and the family community: that frequently, they were large complexes; that various generations housed together; that relatives could form a part; that—as was habitual in antiquity—employees, servants, and slaves also belonged.

To enter in those houses and enkindle in them the light of the peace of the gospel was already an indication from Jesus to his disciples in their mission to Israel (Mark 6:6–13). Paul, like many other missionaries, has conserved the practice, but has internationalized it. The conditions are anything but evident of themselves; the consequences, profound.

One of the conditions is that Christian missionaries, upon arriving with the good news, don't destroy the world they find but baptize it. Everything happens as described by the metaphors of Jesus in the Sermon on the Mount about the salt of the earth and the light of the world. One of the consequences is that the Christian communities don't form as closed circles or parallel societies, but in the midst of the cities and villages where the people have lived before and after their conversion, and that there, in situ, they develop an attraction that grows, impelled by the clarity of the liturgy, the amplitude of the diaconate, and the strength of conviction of the doctrine. The Church, it's true, began small, but in mentality and structure has never been sectarian.

The center and heart is formed by the houses with the Christian families who live in them. Paul advocated them and was not disappointed. It's not, by any means, that the relations were ideal. A fact of no small importance: the women had a difficult time when they had already come to the faith, but not their husbands, who perhaps even wished to distance them from the gospel and its liberating force. Paul says that these women must do all in their power to keep the peace and extend the faith. But he is not blind to the fact that in no way is this something that can be always achieved. Valid then is the principle according to which the freedom of faith has preference; a new union is possible.

Paul also thinks of the children. Already controversial and a subject of debate was the determination of how early an age children or suckling babes could be baptized. In any case, the Apostle is convinced of the beneficial influence that a Christian father or mother can have on a common child, even when one or the other spouse is not Christian. The children are "consecrated" thereby (1 Cor 7:14): they enter into contact with God; the word of God can say something to them; through the love of the parents they are united to the love of God. This positive influence is not at all automatic; nor is there any guarantee to success; faith continues to be grace, and despotism is not love for the children. But good influences exist because families exist.

Christianity is a religion that defines itself starting from Jesus Christ, not by generation, conception, and birth, but by faith and baptism. However, this does not preclude the family factor, but includes it. This is, by far, the most important factor when it's a matter of transmission of the faith. In this aspect, Christianity learned from Judaism and included even pagan families in its theory of success for religious formation. None of the historical and cultural changes in the idea of family has modified anything in this respect. It's not immediately evident that today other methods have to be utilized. Rather, the domestic churches of the beginning remind the large churches of the present that very few are those who have been initiated in the faith, in the love of God and neighbor, and in the hope of eternal life directly by the priest or the bishop, but that for most people it was by their father or their mother (not forgetting the grandparents).

Paul knows many of these houses and families. Some he cites by name. He advocates them—not only he, but he with special emphasis and success. For him it is not only a problem of optimizing missionary strategy or of the best way to encourage and enter into marriage or of the desire for children. It is, rather, a question of positioning before life, before the present life that God gives and before the blessing that he bestows. To know oneself a child of God in a family that forms part of the family of God is a splendid gift.

4

MERCY, JUSTICE, AND LAW

Can Legal Concepts Help Foster New Life?

CATHLEEN KAVENY

⚭

When Pope Francis announced his plans for an Extraordinary Synod on the family, he framed the purpose of the event carefully and decisively. The focus of the Synod is not abstract theoretical questions of moral theology, sacramental theology, and canon law, no matter how important they may be. Instead, its central concerns are concrete and practical: the purpose of the Extraordinary Synod is to "discuss the pastoral challenges of the family in the context of the new evangelization." Pope Francis emphasized that the October 2014 synod was not going to sidestep thorny questions facing the Church today, such as the eligibility of divorced and remarried Catholics to receive the sacrament of the Eucharist. Moreover, he emphasized the importance of approaching these questions within a particular framework appropriate to the Church's mission: "The Church is a mother, and she must travel this path of mercy, and find a form of mercy for all."[1]

In this essay, I would like to contribute to the conversation about this question. In the first section, I will draw upon Cardinal Walter Kasper's book on mercy to develop a richer sense of what mercy means, and what it may require of the Church in its pastoral care for divorced and remarried Catholics. Drawing insights from American civil law, I will address a key objection to Kasper's proposal that most divorced and remarried Catholics cannot be admitted to communion because their sin against the first marriage is a continuing sin. The supreme lawgiver for the Roman Catholic Church is, of course, Jesus Christ, who gave his life in order to give repentant sinners the opportunity for new life. In the brief third section, I reflect upon whether Jesus' teaching is consistent with my proposal.

MERCY AS A NEW CHANCE

What does it mean for the Church to situate its discernment about how to respond to the travails of its members regarding marriage and family life within the framework of mercy? A brilliant and compassionate book written by Cardinal Walter Kasper, *Mercy: The Essence of the Gospel and the Key to Christian Life*, helps us to address this question. Kasper argues that the topic of mercy has been "criminally neglected" in theological reflection, despite the fact that the terrible events of the twentieth century reveal the overwhelming need of humanity for the mercy of God and the mercy of one another.[2] Moreover, Kasper shows that this deepest of human needs corresponds to a fundamental truth about God's nature. God does not merely act mercifully from time to time, God *is* mercy. Kasper writes,

> Thus from the beginning of history, God's counter-action is at work against disaster. From the very

beginning God's merciful action [*Erbarmen*] is powerfully effective. His mercy is how God provides resistance to evil, which is getting the upper hand. He does not do this forcibly and violently; he doesn't simply do battle; rather, in his mercy God repeatedly creates new space for life and for blessing.[3]

Mercy Is God's Defining Attribute

The vision of "new space for life and for blessing" is a key to understanding Kasper's view of divine mercy. While sin entails death, mercy enables new life. God does not merely pronounce forgiveness from a distance, leaving us to stew in our own misery. God gives us a *new chance*, and with it new possibilities for flourishing. As Kasper writes, "In his mercy, God grants humanity life and living space anew."[4] Forgiveness erases the sin; mercy enables new life.

Mercy is not simply one of God's marvelous qualities; according to Kasper, it is God's defining attribute.[5] In fact, mercy is the divine characteristic in light of which all of God's other qualities must be interpreted and understood—including justice.[6]

Moreover, and equally importantly, mercy provides the hermeneutical key to God's relationship with the world; it is nothing other than the "source and goal of God's activity."[7] "God holds the possibility of salvation open for every human being who is fundamentally willing to be converted and who is sorry for his or her guilt, even if their guilt is ever so great and their former life ever so botched up."[8]

Given his view of the nature of God, and the salvific action of Christ, it is not surprising that Kasper views mercy as central to the activity of the Church; in fact, he calls the

Church the "sacrament of love and mercy."[9] Drawing inspiration from Pope John Paul II's beautiful encyclical *Dives in Misericordia*,[10] Kasper argues that the Church must "give witness to divine mercy" in a threefold way: it "must proclaim the mercy of God; it must concretely provide people God's mercy in the sacrament of mercy, the sacrament of reconciliation; and it must allow God's mercy to appear and be realized in its concrete structures, its entire life, and even in its laws."[11]

It is not enough, therefore, for the Church to proclaim God's mercy with words, or even to make God's mercy available through the sacrament of reconciliation. As the body of Christ, it must incarnate God's mercy in all aspects of its institutional life, including in its canon law. It must not cater to the respectable, the proper, and the prosperous. Like Jesus himself, it must reach out lovingly to the poor and the marginalized, especially to sinners. Kasper writes; "The most serious criticism that can be leveled against the church, therefore, is the accusation that oftentimes only a few deeds follow, or appear to follow, its words. The church is reproached for speaking of God's mercy, while it is perceived by many people to be strict, harsh, and pitiless."[12]

Kasper emphasizes that mercy does not undermine justice, but it fulfills and transcends it. It does this, not by denying that a wrong occurred, but by refusing to allow the wrong act to entirely define the wrongdoer, and resisting any effort to do justice by annihilating all hope of that person's future participation in the community.

Furthermore, canon law itself must be concerned with mercy, because mercy is part of canon law's ultimate purpose: fostering the Church's active participation in God's saving plan for humanity. Prioritizing mercy in the interpretation of canon law, however, does not mean abandoning the law's objective character. Instead, we might say, part of the task of mercy is to invite us to fine-tune the application of the law, by using the *aequitas canonica*. "The point is to apply the objective sense of the legislation analogously in an often complex concrete situation so that the law's application is truly fair and just in the given situation."[13] Moreover, he emphasizes that canon law must be interpreted in particular cases "according to its authentic intention, that is, according to the οἰκονομία, the entire divine order of salvation."[14] Concretely, that means leaving people room for a new start and hope for a better future: "The judge will then render a fair judgment, but nevertheless not a judgment that functions like a guillotine, but rather a judgment that leaves open 'a loophole of mercy,' that is, that makes possible a new beginning for the other, if he or she is of good will."[15]

Mercy and the Family

In his recent lecture on "The Gospel of the Family," Cardinal Kasper expanded upon his thoughts about the relationship of mercy, justice, and law to particular questions facing the Extraordinary Synod, such as how the church deals with divorced and remarried individuals.[16] Cautioning against reducing the problem to one of readmittance to communion, he stresses that the Church must consider "pastoral care for marriage and family life in their totality," which must include thoroughgoing catechesis and marriage preparation beginning adolescence.[17] Prevention of family breakdown, however important it may be, is not enough in today's situation. Kasper observes that "many deserted partners, for the sake of the children, are dependent upon a new partnership and a civil marriage, which they cannot again quit without new guilt. In such new ties they often experience human happiness—indeed a virtual gift from heaven—after previous bitter experiences."[18]

How should the Church respond to such couples? On the one hand, Kasper recognizes that "it cannot propose a solution apart from or contrary to Jesus' words," which form the basis for the Church's teaching on the indissolubility of sacramental marriage.[19] On the other hand, Kasper cannot interpret Jesus' words apart from the entire context of Jesus' saving mission: "Mercy and fidelity belong together. Therefore, there can be no human solution that is absolutely desperate and hopeless. However far a human being may fall, he or she never falls deeper than God's mercy can reach."[20] For Kasper, this point is crucial. God's mercy is creative; it entails the opportunity for renewed life, especially included is a renewed and richer relationship with God.

With these principles firmly in place, Kasper proceeds with caution to the analysis of particular cases, which he divides into two categories: 1) situations in which the parties are convinced that their first sacramental marriage was invalid, and 2) situations in which the first sacramental marriage was valid, but proved intractably unworkable. With respect to situations in the first category, he calls for revision to the Church's annulment practices and procedures, so that they better honor the personal dignity of those who participate in them, since "behind every process, behind every case stand persons who expect justice."[21]

It is Kasper's response to situations in the second category, however, that has generated the most attention and controversy. Kasper begins by pointing out that civilly divorced and remarried Catholics have been encouraged to receive spiritual communion at Mass, despite their irregular marital status. He then goes on to ask why they should be excluded from actual receipt of the Eucharist. "If we exclude divorced and remarried Christians, who are properly disposed, from the sacraments and refer them to the extrasacramental way of salvation, do we not then place the fundamental sacramental structure of the Church in question?"[22] Allowing such persons to receive communion, Kasper emphasizes, does not mean that divorced and remarried persons can contract a second sacramental marriage during the lifetime of their first spouse. It is not a "second ship" after the shipwreck of their first marriage. It is, however, a "lifesaving plank" that is mercifully extended to a drowning person—"a plank of salvation through participation in communion."[23]

What does it mean for a divorced and remarried person to be "properly disposed" to receive communion? Kasper is no latitudinarian; a careful reading of his proposal reveals that he sets five criteria for the reception of communion: 1) the divorced Catholic is sincerely sorry that he or she failed in the first marriage; 2) a return to the first marriage is definitely out of the question; 3) the second marriage cannot be abandoned without incurring new guilt; 4) the Catholic seeking communion tries to live out the second marriage in the context of faith, including raising any children as Catholics; and 5) the Catholic longs for the sacraments of penance and communion as a source of strength.[24]

Under these conditions, Kasper proposes that the penitent, divorced, and remarried Catholic ought to be admitted to confession and communion. He says with passion as well as rhetorical power, "If forgiveness is possible for the murderer, then it is also possible for the adulterer." The sacraments, he reminds us, are not "a reward for good conduct or for an elite, who exclude those who are most in need of them."[25] Despite its power, this rhetorical question has met with significant resistance among some moralists and canonists.[26] Because a sacramental marriage endures until the death of one of the parties, Kasper's critics insist that the Church must treat the purported second marriage as entailing repeated acts of adultery. Consequently, they maintain that Kasper's analogy is inapt: the repentant murderer confesses a sin that is over and done with, while the divorced and remarried person confesses a sin that is ongoing and continuing, without a firm purpose of amendment. Consequently, the murderer is eligible for absolution, while the divorced and remarried person is not—unless he or she agrees to live with his second spouse without engaging in a sexual relationship. In short, Cardinal Kasper's critics believe that his proposal for readmitting divorced and remarried Catholics to communion is false mercy, because it does not take into account the demands of truth and justice.

SKETCHING A WAY FORWARD: INSIGHTS FROM THE CIVIL LAW

Is there a way out of this conundrum? In the remainder of this chapter, I would like to propose a possible path, composed of two steps. First, I would like to suggest that the term *adultery*, as it is used in the contemporary context, is not the proper way in which to describe the sin of a divorced and civilly remarried person against his or her sacramental first marriage. Second, I do not mean to deny that in many cases, the parties to a broken marriage have sinned against each other and their bond of matrimony. I would like to suggest, however, that it is possible to treat their sins against the first marriage as completed sin, and not as ongoing sin. By treating them in this way, it is possible for the divorced parties to a sacramental marriage to repent of their wrongdoing, and to begin a new life with a new spouse. It is possible for them to have a merciful second chance.

Before I proceed down this path, I would like to express a few caveats. I fully recognize that my approach may be somewhat novel. I am presenting it as a thought experiment. I am inspired, in all humility, by Pope Francis's own call for new thinking on these matters in order to address real pastoral problems. I hope that my approach is consistent with the deepest insights of the tradition, and in particular with the account of the relationship of God's mercy and God's justice, as articulated so eloquently by Cardinal Kasper. My goal, in fact, is to show in some detail how mercy might be made compatible with the operations of legal justice in these instances. But I am very much open to critique and correction.

I hope to encourage the refinement of the Church's legal terms and norms, by pressing the Catholic community to think more precisely about the nature and timing of the wrong that is done to a sacramental marriage by a divorce and remarriage. At first glance, the technical legal terms I will use in my discussion will seem very improbable tools for advancing the work of mercy. My hope, however, is that more precise use of legal terms may help us to see how the Church's application of mercy in the case of divorced and remarried Catholics does not undermine justice. As Cardinal Kasper noted, one way in which mercy supports justice is by encouraging a more careful fit between our legal categories and the complicated factual situations to which they apply. It is "not a matter of an arbitrary reinterpretation, but rather a matter of bringing to bear the sense of the objective law in a way that is appropriate to the matter at hand and to the situation."[27]

Although I am not a canon lawyer, I am an American civil lawyer. While I am drawing upon concepts and cases from American law, they are not idiosyncratically American. They point to issues that need to be addressed by every legal system.[28] Like the legal tradition of the Church, secular legal traditions also must strive to apply legal-moral concepts such to particular situations involving fallible human beings. While the concept of mercy may not explicitly animate aspects of secular law to the degree they animate canon law, we will see that secular judges do take into consideration the needs of human beings to move on with their lives without living under the constant threat of legal prosecution. In a sense, then, they are sensitive to mercy's demand for a new start. As the participants in the synod address the changing circumstances of marriage (which is a matter of natural morality and civil law as well as canon law and sacramental theology), therefore, they may find that civil law provides a helpful touchstone for the discussion.

Is "Adultery" the Right Concept?

The concept of adultery—and the wrong it works—has changed significantly over the centuries. In ancient times, adultery was generally seen to be analogous to a property crime—the violation of another man's property in a woman. In Mosaic Law, as in early Roman law, a married man who had sexual relations with an unmarried woman was not committing adultery. This activity was problematic not only in itself, but also in its consequences for the social and economic structure of the household. It rendered the lines of patrilineal succession uncertain, since a man would not be certain that any children borne by his wife actually belonged to him.

In our own era in the West, the concept of adultery refers centrally to the betrayal of one spouse by another. It applies equally to men and women. The sexual betrayal is one aspect of the phenomenon of adultery—but it is only one aspect. Adultery involves a multifaceted betrayal. While purporting to maintain a joint household and family life, the adulterous spouse is in fact diverting his or her sexual intimacy, emotional support, and perhaps even financial resources away from the joint project of the marriage. In the central case of adultery, the adulterer's behavior is often kept a secret from the other spouse, who often feels shamed and duped when the betrayal is discovered. Moreover, the betrayed spouse often experiences a sense of being used by the betraying spouse. While his or her partner has been looking outside the marriage for satisfaction, the betrayed spouse has been devoting his or her attention and energies to the marital partnership. Particularly if the innocent spouse is a woman who devotes herself to taking care of young children rather than participating in the work force, she is relying upon the marriage for her financial security and material well-being. In our era, then adultery involves three factors: 1) deceit; 2) physical and emotional betrayal; and 3) exploitation of the innocent spouse.[29]

It seems to me, therefore, that the term *adultery* does not rightly apply to a situation that arises *after* a married couple obtains a civil divorce and one or both parties remarry. Civil divorce is public; there is no deceit involved. Because the divorce dissolves the legal bond between the two parties to the original marriage, what happens after that point does not count as betrayal, strictly speaking. Finally, the divorce has put each party on notice that the other is no longer engaged in building a common life with the other. It has put both parties on notice that they have no expectation of sexual fidelity from each other. After a civil divorce, therefore, it is very difficult to think of even the innocent party as still *exploited* by his or her former spouse.

So I think that it is deeply misleading to speak of one person acting "adulterously" toward his or her first spouse after they have been civilly divorced, because using that term in this situation it does not account for key elements of the term's meaning. It is even more misleading, I think, to speak of a person who is divorced and remarried as committing adultery against his first spouse when having sexual relations with his new spouse.

At this point, I need to emphasize two key points. First, it may very well be the case that one or both parties acted wrongly in bringing about the breakdown of their marriage. But once there is no realistic possibility for reconciliation in this lifetime, the wrong is a completed wrong, not a continuing wrong. Catholics, after all, do not believe that marriage extends into eternity. A marriage as a joint project between two people is over, therefore, when there is no possibility of it being revived in this life. Consequently, the wrongs committed by marriage partners against that marriage are completed once they are civilly divorced, and it is clear that their relationship is no longer salvageable.

Second, it is still possible to act wrongfully against one's former spouse after the divorce. It is not as if the divorce entirely erases the bond between the two parties. One party may, for example, have a moral obligation to pay alimony to support the other party, particularly if he or she dedicated his or her time to raising children. Every parent has continuing moral obligations, I believe, not only to the children, but also to their mother or father—one's former spouse. At the very least, and in all circumstances, I think that both parties have a continuing obligation to pray for their former spouses.

Neither of these two points, however, entails the claim that a divorced person commits a *further* wrong against his or her first spouse—or against his or her first marriage—by remarrying. By disentangling their lives, by separating each other with respect to bed and board, the civil divorce has made it clear that their joint marital project is finished and not to be resumed in this lifetime—or ever, since we know there is no marriage in heaven. When one or both parties remarry, they make new commitments to different people. But in and of itself, that new commitment does not do further harm to the first marriage. Because the first marriage cannot be revivified in this life, it is no longer susceptible to any further damage. Consequently, it accords with the facts about marital life today in the West to think, Cardinal Kasper suggests, that the parties to the first marriage can repent of any harm they have done, and move on with their lives, grateful for God's forgiveness and mercy.

Defining the Offense

As a legal tradition matures, it adds nuance and complexity to its categories of offense, in order to better account for salient features of the cases it encounters. Consider, for example, the development in the crime of homicide in the Anglo-American tradition. As late as the eleventh century, all homicide was either murder or justifiable homicide. All murder was punishable by death. As time went on, distinctions were added to the law to save the less culpable "murderers" (e.g., those who had killed accidentally). Initially, ameliorating the sentence of such criminals was a matter of the king's favor. Later, as the law itself began to incorporate the categories that triggered a royal pardon, it became a matter of justice to treat intentional homicide different from accidental killing.[30]

So a legal system can and does develop over time to take into account morally salient factors. As the example of murder shows, this development can happen as society comes to a better understanding of the difference made by the mental state of the criminal (the *mens rea*). But development can also take place as society comes to a better understanding of the exact nature and scope of the wrong that it is targeting (the *actus reus*).

The first task facing any prosecutor is to determine the "unit of prosecution" for the wrong committed by the defendant.[31] This task is not always easy. Does a thief who takes six bracelets off one dresser commit one crime or six? Does a father who hits his child with all his force three times commit one crime or three? Determining the answer to these questions requires attention to the purpose of the lawmaker. But it also requires courts to exercise practical wisdom, because legislative intent is not always clear. The challenge in defining the crime is more difficult when what is at stake is not merely an isolated action, but an organized pattern of behavior. For example, one might ask if operating an illegal tavern is one offense, or if the offenses mount up with every drink poured or customer served.[32]

What, exactly, is the wrong committed by the divorced and remarried Catholic? The Catholic tradition has generally said that such a person commits adultery every time he or she has sexual relations with the second spouse. Although adultery was not widely criminalized in Europe, some American states, influenced as they were by Puritan moral codes, did make it a crime. In many cases, American courts did indeed see each act of adultery as a separate chargeable offense. And in many circumstances, that might make sense. But in circumstances involving longer-term second relationships (such as involved in divorced and remarried Catholics), some American courts reframed the charge so that it better fit the actual offense.

Consider, for example, the case of *Ex parte Snow*, in which the Supreme Court of the United States was asked to grapple with the question of how Mormon polygamy intersected with the laws against unlawful cohabitation.[33] Lorenzo Snow was a polygamist living in Utah. The federal prosecutor charged him with three counts of unlawful cohabitation for three successive calendar years. The court held that the government could not arbitrarily divide a single, uninterrupted, three-year unlawful cohabitation into three separate criminal charges; the description of the crime needed to conform to the lived reality of the defendant.

A second polygamy case makes the point even more clearly. In *Ex parte Nielsen*, the federal government charged Hans Nielsen with unlawful cohabitation and the separate crime of adultery. Rejecting the government's way of framing Nielsen's criminal activity, the United States Supreme Court held that adultery was the lesser crime included within the crime of cohabitation.[34] The court looked at the big picture: it recognized that the problem raised by the Mormon polygamy cases was not only, or mainly, the sex outside the first marriage considered in the abstract. For the American legal system, the fundamental problem was the fact that Mormon men saw themselves as entering an additional marital relationship, of which the sexual acts were only one part.

As *Ex parte Snow* and *Ex parte Nielsen* illustrate, one very ordinary challenge of every legal system is to describe the wrongful activity engaged in by the defendants in the right way—in a way that captures what they are actually doing, as human beings and moral agents. In some cases, properly describing the defendant's wrongful action requires looking beyond the isolated, individual acts they have committed, and situating them within a broader pattern of purposeful activity. It requires, so to speak, recalibrating the focus of the law's lens to get a meaningful perspective on the scene.

It seems to me that this sort of recalibration of perspective could assist the Church in understanding the situation of divorced and remarried persons. The proper description of their activity is committed *cohabitation*—it is simply inaccurate to portray a civilly divorced and remarried Catholic as engaged in multiple, disconnected, acts of adultery. The parties to the second marriage are not skulking off to a hotel room to grasp a moment of irresponsible pleasure. They are engaged in an ongoing, committed, and organized life project, which includes but is not limited to sexual relations. That life project may very well involve further, ancillary commitments to children, to aging family members, and to one another in sickness and health.

In some respects, both moralists and jurists face the same challenge. In order to do their jobs well, both of them need to frame the question appropriately. They need to ask, What is the proper description of the activity we are charged with guiding and regulating? For the Catholic Church, at this moment in time, the issue at stake in the case of divorced and remarried persons is not primarily about sexual acts. Most fundamentally, it is about relinquishing one complex set of commitments and vulnerabilities that marriage brings, and taking upon a new set of commitments and vulnerabilities, even while one's first spouse is still living. As the judgment in *Ex parte Nielsen* intimates, the broader frame provided by the new relationship should be the focus of our attention and analysis.

At this point in my essay, a reader might object that my insights from American law may be interesting, but they do not advance Cardinal Kasper's case for mercy for the divorced and remarried. In fact, some readers might claim that I am harming his case. Rather than saying that divorced and remarried persons sin in each and every sexual act they commit, my legal analysis commits me to saying that they sin in the totality of their cohabitation in the second marriage. If anything, that puts them in a worse position, since if that is the case, they cannot even remedy their situation even by living together as brother and sister.

My response to this objection is to turn to civil law for further insight. With respect to the situation of the divorced and remarried, in addition to addressing the question, "What is the wrong at stake?" we also need to ask, "When does the wrong at stake begin and when does it end?" Does the wrong actually continue as long as the second marital relationship continues, provided the first spouse is still alive?

Not surprisingly, secular law has had to grapple with the general question of how long an offense continues in a number of cases. As we will see, the law recognizes that the mere fact that the effects of an offense persist throughout some length of time does not make it a "continuing offense." I think this recognition will provide some assistance to Kasper's approach. If an offense is completed, and therefore not continuing from a legal or moral perspective, its agent can repent of it effectively. To put it more concretely: if a man or woman's acts of wrongdoing against his or her first marriage are completed (say) at the time he or she contracts a second marriage, then he or she can effectively repent of those acts of wrongdoing and receive communion.[35]

Continuing versus Completed Offenses

As I noted above, a key barrier to admitting divorced and civilly remarried persons to communion is the canonical judgment that their offense against the first sacramental marriage is a continuing offense. According to critics of Cardinal Kasper's proposal, it is this fact that distinguishes the situation of the murderer from that of the divorced and remarried person with respect to communion. The murder is completed; therefore the murderer can repent of his or her sin and receive the Eucharist. The divorced and remarried person cannot, because the sin is ongoing, rather than completed.

But why do we have to think of the situation in this way? Answering this question requires us to explore a more fundamental issue: How do we distinguish between completed wrongs, on the one hand, and continuing wrongs, on the other? A moment's thought reveals that the answer to that question is not self-evident. Why not, for example, view the murder as a continuing wrong? After all, the victim continues to be dead, and the suffering that loss inflicts upon his family, friends, and community continues for years. Why do not we say, for example, that the murder is an offense that continues for the expected lifetime of the victim?

As it turns out, the civil legal system recognizes that distinguishing instantaneous from continuous offenses is not always a simple and straightforward task.[36] Generally speaking, an instantaneous offense is a "discrete act" that occurs at a particular moment in time. The harm that it causes occurs in that moment, and does not extend beyond it. A continuing offense differs in two ways: First, it generally involves an ongoing course of conduct. Second, the harm it causes persists over that period of time. *Both* prongs are necessary to the definition of a continuing offense. Consequently, the law recognizes that some conduct that counts as an ongoing course of criminal activity does not actually qualify as a continuing offense. "The hallmark of the continuing offense is that it purdures beyond the initial illegal act, and that 'each day brings a renewed threat of the evil Congress sought to prevent' even after the elements necessary to establish the crime have occurred."[37] At the same time, the courts have recognized that even "continuing offenses do not, in general, continue indefinitely."[38]

It is important to understand what constitutes a continuing offense for the sake of conceptual clarity. It is also important for ancillary reasons, such as determining how to apply the statute of limitations for a crime. The longer a crime continues, the longer a potential defendant will be at risk of prosecution. There are obviously competing values at stake in deciding how long a potential defendant should be vulnerable to state action; it is in the struggle of courts to reconcile those values that we can see some resonances with Kasper's notion of mercy. The courts recognize, for example, that statutes of limitations not only encourage efficiency and accuracy in prosecution, but also protect the defendant's rights. Moreover, the courts actively favor the value of "repose," which scholar Jeffrey Boles defines as consisting of the "interrelated concepts of affording peace of mind, avoiding the disruption of settled expectations, and reducing uncertainty about the future in the lives of defendants."[39] By favoring the concept of repose, then, the courts recognize the need for parties to be able to move on with their lives, and (except in the case of very serious crimes, such as murder), not to be forever haunted by past mistakes. We can see here resonances of Kasper's understanding of the purpose of mercy.

In the United States, no uniform approach existed to the definition of continuing offenses for many years. In 1970, however, the United States Supreme Court addressed the matter in *Toussie v. United States*.[40] Robert Toussie was required to register for the draft within five days of his eighteenth birthday, which occurred in 1959. He never registered with a draft board at any time, despite the fact that the law required every American man aged eighteen to twenty-six to do so. Toussie was indicted for evading the draft in 1967, and subsequently convicted of the crime. Toussie argued on appeal that the indictment was barred by the five-year statute of limitations. In response, the U.S. government argued that the crime continued every day that he did not register until he reached age twenty-six.

The U.S. Supreme Court sided with the defendant, and reversed his conviction.[41] The court set out a two-pronged test to identify continuing crimes. First, courts are to look at the intention of the lawmaker: Does the legislature intend to define the wrong as a continuing wrong or not? Second, courts are to look at the nature of the crime. The key factor here is whether the offense features "a harm that lasts as long as that course of conduct persists."[42] Precisely because it works a greater disadvantage to the defendant, the Supreme Court maintains that there is a strong presumption against finding an offense to be continuing rather than completed.

So, for example, conspiracy, sometimes called a "criminal combination," is widely considered to be the paradigmatic continuing offense—two or more parties gather, often in secret, to plan other crimes. A conspiracy to rob banks, therefore, is a crime that is distinct from and additional to the specific robberies themselves. It continues until it is broken up by a distinct act, such as one of the coconspirators going to the police to blow the whistle on his former partners, or the police making an arrest. A criminal conspiracy is a powder keg of future criminal activity. Kidnapping is also generally seen as a continuing offense. "This is a crime of continuing force upon the person...while parents and family are kept in a constant state of anxiety."[43] Possession of prohibited items is also widely seen as a continuing offense. The very fact that dangerous and illegal items, such as bombs or drugs, are ready at hand, threatens the well-being of the community at large.

It is important to emphasize that one cannot draw the conclusion that an offense is a "continuing offense" simply because some of its aspects or effects carry on through time. The term *continuing offense* is a technical legal term, not merely a chronological term. The underlying situation in the *Toussie* case makes that fact abundantly clear. Although

Robert Toussie was out of compliance with the draft registration requirement from five days after his eighteenth birthday until the time he turned twenty-six, the Supreme Court held that the actual offense was completed when he failed to register five days after his eighteenth birthday.

To qualify as a continuing offense, from a legal perspective, the wrongdoing must involve continuing, legally cognizable harm. It is this point that helps us see why the better decisions have not treated every kind of extended, wrongful possession as a continuing offense.[44] For example, in *United States v. De La Mata*, the United States Court of Appeals for the 11th Circuit held that bank fraud is *not* a continuing offense.[45] The defendants had entered into fraudulent lease agreements, collecting payment on the leases until they were discovered and stopped by law enforcement agents. The prosecution maintained that the defendants were engaged in a continuing offense that did not terminate until they were caught. The court disagreed: "Taken to its logical conclusion, the collection of rents on a lease obtained by fraud, for a term of 99 years, would toll the statute of limitations for 99 years. We think this goes too far."[46] The court distinguished between the crime, which was the fraudulent scheme itself, and the working out through time of that crime, which was the collection of lease payments over the course of the lease term. The lesson of the *De La Mata* case, then, is this: simply because the rollout of the crime took place over time does not mean that the crime itself was a continuing offense from a legal perspective. Unlike possession of dangerous weapons, the mere servicing of a fraudulent lease does not pose any further ongoing dangers to the community.

It seems to me that the secular law on continuing offenses offers lessons that can be applied by analogy to the situation of divorced and remarried Catholics in two ways. First, in deciding whether or not an offense meets the technical legal definition of a continuing offense, the courts focus on whether the harm the law is designed to prevent continues throughout time. Let us assume for the sake of argument that a divorced person who has remarried has inflicted some wrong upon their first marriage. Is it correct, really, to say that that harm to the original spouse, their children, and the community continues to pile up indefinitely, year upon year? In the majority of cases, it seems to me that this is not the case. The harm is completed with the dissolution of the first marriage, and all that it entails, such as the separation of one household into two households. One could argue that the second marriage ceremony causes some additional harm, as it is a definitive sign that the first marriage has no chance of being revivified. But assuming that the divorce and remarriage did harm the first marriage, the harm does not extend throughout the second marriage. In fact, it may well be the case that the relationship between the parties to the original marriage is stabilized, and the well-being of their children is enhanced, if they both move on to stable second relationships. The parties to the sacramental marriage may be able to see each other without bitterness, if they move on to partnerships in which they can flourish.

Second, the case law suggests that we might do well to adopt the distinction between the offense itself, on the one hand, and living out the consequences of the event, on the other. The current Catholic moral and canonical approach treats each sexual act in the second marriage as an ongoing betrayal of the first marriage—as the signposts of a continuing offense. In my judgment, this way of framing the situation is significantly distorted. In contrast, I think the life of the second marriage, including its sexual relationship, is best seen as a living out of the second wedding ceremony, which in most cases decisively ends the possibility of the resumption of the first marriage.[47]

DISCERNING THE INTENT OF THE LAWMAKER—WHAT DID JESUS SAY AND DO?

All of the secular legal cases I discuss above make one important point: the intent of the legislator is a crucial factor in determining the nature and duration of an offense. The courts do not deny that it is within the power of a legislature to frame an offense as a continuing offense. Given the countervailing values, especially the value of repose, they insist that the intent of the legislature be clear before finding a particular offense to be a continuing offense.

Within the Catholic community, the supreme lawgiver is God, as most perfectly revealed in Jesus Christ. What did Jesus teach regarding divorce and remarriage? While a full examination of this topic is beyond the scope of this chapter, I think it is necessary to make a few observations.[48]

First, it is important to pay attention to the social context in which Jesus spoke. Divorce was a near-universal phenomenon in the ancient Near East, including among ancient Jews. As the distinguished New Testament scholar John P. Meier has pointed out, "Almost all the pre-70 Jewish texts known to us reflect a Judaism in which a man could divorce his wife for practically any reason."[49] The reverse was not true; in ancient Palestine, a woman could not divorce her husband for *any* reason. Furthermore, a divorced woman was in an extraordinarily precarious position in ancient societies; unless she could find another man to marry, she would be dependent upon her own family of birth to take her in and protect her.[50]

In Luke and Matthew, therefore, the accounts of Jesus' statements on divorce reflect the vast disparity in power and vulnerability between husband and wife. It is the *man* who divorces his wife and marries another who commits adultery, and (in Matthew) *causes* his former wife to be involved in adultery. The moral fault is primarily his, not hers. In sharp contrast, Mark's Gospel and Paul's First Letter to the Corinthians also make the additional claim that a woman who divorces her husband commits adultery. Most commentators point out that the Gospel of Mark and Paul's First Letter to the Corinthians were written in the context of a Roman legal system, in which women as well as men had the legal right to divorce their spouses. Because this was not even an option for ordinary Jewish women in Jesus' era, Meier concludes that the words of Mark 10:12 "almost automatically fall out of consideration as a saying coming from the historical Jesus."[51]

Is it logical to extend Jesus' words condemning divorce from a Palestinian context in which men can unilaterally divorce their vulnerable wives, to a Roman context in which women are more equal, and can also divorce their husbands? It depends, in my view, upon the point of the prohibition of divorce and remarriage. If the purpose is primarily to protect sexual purity, then the extension seems valid. If the purpose is to protect vulnerable people, especially vulnerable women, then the extension is more questionable, at least in some cases. As Jesus' conduct throughout Scripture reveals, the main concern is not to promote purity, but instead to protect the vulnerable.

Second, it is important to pay attention to the audience to whom Jesus is speaking. The fullest Synoptic account of Jesus' views on marriage and divorce are found in Mark 10:1–12. Jesus addresses the question in an academic way; we are told at the beginning of that passage that Jesus "left that place and went to the region of Judea and beyond the Jordan. And crowds again gathered around him; and, as was his custom, he again taught them. Some Pharisees came, and to test him they asked, "Is it lawful for a man to divorce his wife?" (Mark 10:1–2).

In response to the Pharisees, who pointed to Moses' permission for Jewish men to divorce their wives (for any reason), Jesus invokes God's original intention for marriage:

> He answered them, "What did Moses command you?" They said, "Moses allowed a man to write a certificate of dismissal and to divorce her." But Jesus said to them, "Because of your hardness of heart he wrote this commandment for you. But from the beginning of creation, 'God made them male and female.' 'For this reason a man shall leave his father and mother and be joined to his wife, and the two shall become one flesh.' So they are no longer two, but one flesh. Therefore what God has joined together, let no one separate." (Mark 10:6–9)

Jesus is here giving an academic response to an academic question, posed by powerful and potentially hostile questioners who were "testing" him. Given their authority in the

Jewish community, the Pharisees saw themselves in a position not only to test Jesus, but also to judge him. Because their view on divorce was aligned with that of Moses, the Pharisees assumed that it was aligned with God's own will regarding marriage. In his rejoinder, Jesus not only conveyed God's true position on marriage; he also demonstrated his own rank relative to Moses. Jesus claimed his own authority as the paramount interpreter of Jewish law. [52]

In his conversation with the Pharisees, therefore, Jesus was engaged in what we today would call an academic discussion with those who purported to be his equals or superiors in authority. He was not dealing with a pastoral situation that called upon him to apply his teaching to particular human persons dealing with the consequences of human sin. Scripture also provides us with examples of Jesus' activity as a merciful healer, which helps us situate his more academic discussion of marriage in a broader context.

The story that I find most helpful here is that of Jesus' encounter with the Samaritan woman at Jacob's well (John 4:1–42). Jesus asks her for a drink, which astonished her, because Jews normally disdained interaction with Samaritans. In return, she asked him for the living water that only he could provide. The story continues:

> Jesus said to her, "Go, call your husband, and come back." The woman answered him, "I have no husband." Jesus said to her, "You are right in saying, 'I have no husband'; for you have had five husbands, and the one you have now is not your husband. What you have said is true!" (John 4:16–18)

Jesus reveals himself to the Samaritan woman as the Messiah. He reveals to her a great mystery: that he is the source of the waters of eternal life, and calls upon her to "worship the Father in spirit and truth." Yet Jesus does not impose a rigid, legal response upon her obviously irregular marital situation. Jesus does not tell her to return to her first husband, provided he is still living. He does not instruct her to leave her current consort. In short, he deals pastorally and constructively with the woman. He does not treat her situation in the same abstract manner that he conducted his academic discussion about marriage and divorce with the Pharisees.

Instead, Jesus makes creative use of the Samaritan woman's situation, turning her into a disciple and a partner in his ongoing work of evangelization. He told her the truth about her situation; but he did it in love, in a way that made her marvel at his insight. And the truth was life-giving, not only to her, but to her entire community. "Many Samaritans from that city believed in him because of that women's testimony, 'He told me everything I have ever done'" (John 4:39). He used his knowledge of her sins, not to condemn her to death, but to convert others to new life.

The Gospel of John also highlights the merciful tenderness in Jesus' treatment of sinners, in contrast with the sharpness that characterizes his more academic battles with religious teachers (John 8:1–11). Seeking to trap Jesus yet again, the Pharisees used a woman caught in adultery as the bait. They brought her to Jesus, asking whether they should stone her in accordance with the Law of Moses. Jesus not only evades the academic trap, but also places himself pastorally squarely on the side of the terrified woman. He responds to their query by brilliantly deflecting its force: "Let anyone among you who is without sin be the first to throw a stone at her" (John 8:7). Everyone else drifts away, leaving Jesus alone with the woman. Yet the only sinless man does not condemn her, but tells her, "Go your way, and from now on do not sin again" (John 8:11).

It is worth thinking about what Jesus' admonition means. Would he require her, for example, to leave a second husband whom she had married after her first husband divorced her? But why would Jesus deflect the death-dealing legalism of the Pharisees only to impose an even more rigorous form of legalism upon her conscience? In my view, for Jesus to tell the woman caught in adultery to "go and sin no more" means that it must be *possible* for her to go and sin no more—and to *continue to live*, in the time, circumstances, and culture in which she found herself. Otherwise, his efforts to save her from execution would be pointless and cruel.

Finally, it is important to pay attention to the overarching purpose of the law. No particular legal provision is self-interpreting; it must be understood and applied with reference to the good of the community it purports to guide and to serve. Jesus regularly reminds us that the commands and prohibitions of the Torah must be situated in a broader context. Confronting him with yet another test, a Pharisee asks him which commandment is the greatest; Jesus responds,

> "'You shall love the Lord your God with all your heart, and with all your soul, and with all your mind.' This is the greatest and first commandment. And a second is like it: 'You shall love your neighbor as yourself.' On these two commandments hang all the law and the prophets." (Matt 22:37–40)

As Walter Kasper has shown so well, the God whom we are to love is the God of mercy, the God who wills to save all human beings. We must therefore interpret Jesus' words about marriage and divorce in light of that overarching truth. It is clear that Jesus rejects divorce and remarriage as contrary to the original will of God. It is clear that he treats a man's divorce and remarriage as akin to adultery, and that from the earliest times in the Christian community, that judgment has been extended to a woman's divorce and remarriage. But nothing in Jesus' words or conduct demands that the sin involved in divorce and remarriage must be treated as a sin that continues indefinitely, without possibility of effective repentance as long as one's first spouse is still alive. To impose such a requirement in every case is not merciful, and mercy is the ultimate touchstone for the divine lawgiver.

A NEXT STEP: REFLECTIONS ON SACRAMENTAL MARRIAGE

The core of my argument can be summarized in this fashion: The parties to a failed first marriage may very well have harmed each other and that marriage during the course of their breakup and its immediate aftermath. In most cases, the contracting of a second civil marriage completely extinguishes any hope of reconciliation of the parties to the first marriage in this lifetime. Since there is no marrying or giving in marriage in heaven, the harm the parties have done to their first marriage is completed, not ongoing. Therefore, they should be able to repent of that harm and move on to fulfill the new responsibilities of their second marriage.

I have not addressed, however, one key objection. Someone might say that my analysis might be all well and good for natural marriage, but does not accommodate the special concerns of sacramental marriage, which the Church teaches is indissoluble. Addressing those concerns in detail is beyond the scope of this essay. I will however, make a few brief points.

Note that the sharp distinction between natural and sacramental marriage is not supported by the biblical texts. It is an innovation of the canonical tradition itself. My own view is that it should be possible to see the bond created by the first sacramental marriage as continuing in some way (e.g., in the obligations of the parties to pray for each other), while not interpreting that continuing sacramental bond as excluding a second, natural marriage. Does the Church have the power to develop its doctrine of sacramental marriage in this way, in favor of mercy? I believe so. In fact, there is precedent for such development within the tradition itself.

As John T. Noonan Jr., the great historian of the canon law of marriage, has pointed out, the canonical tradition has long balanced a number of values in both its definition of marriage and in its articulation of its key characteristics:

> The union of the baptized was the symbol of the union of Christ and his Church, as, in another way, the marriage of a bishop to his see was its symbol. The curia had dissolved both sorts of unions by means of a power put above the human and had stopped short only of formally dissolving the carnal unions of the baptized. For eight centuries of legal process, however, even the symbolic values of these unions had been balanced against other values in

the system. Neither the theoretical construct of what nature demanded in marriage nor the express texts of Scripture, neither the absence of precedent nor the desire for uniformity, had barred innovation by the creative lawyers of the past. Variety in the unions already recognized—in their purposes, their stability, their manner of termination, their symbolism was the ground which justified the belief that the last class of marriage had not been created.[53]

5

THE FUTURE OF THE FAMILY FROM A CHRISTIAN PERSPECTIVE

WALTER KASPER

∾

THE NEW SITUATION AS A CHALLENGE

At first sight the theological and pastoral reflections on the theme of family indicate a contradictory result.[1] Normally, the majority of children and youth today still grow up in a family, and in the family they receive the fundamental imprint for life. According to surveys, the majority of young people today also look for their life happiness in a stable union of man and woman with children. On the other hand, the number of divorces and family separations and, as a consequence, the number of those who fail to realize their life project has increased dramatically. The number of those who back off, fearful of marriage or founding a family, has likewise grown: or they practice other forms of life and family (single-parent families, reconstituted families, nonconjugal life communities, homosexual life communities, or individual existences).

The change is profound. Many understand it simply as a crisis of the idea of family. The student of the cultural history of the family will adopt a more cautious attitude. The family is *the* originating structure of human culture. And, in effect, in differentiated forms, it is found in the diverse cultures and epochs. It goes back to the very beginnings of humanity and is present in all known cultures. It is at the service of the reproduction of the respective lineage or race, the transmission of culture and religion, development, protection, assistance, and care of the individual. What today we understand by "nuclear-family," in the sense of family composed of father-mother-children, was originally inserted in the extended family and domestic community formed by various generations, together with more distant relatives and servants. This form of marriage, as the life community of a man and a woman together with their children, often qualified as bourgeois, began to emancipate from the primitive extended family only from the eighteenth century and, in the context of the present social changes, has entered into profound transformation and crisis.

The causes of this change are multiple. It is necessary to guard against hasty moral evaluations. Many millions of people find themselves in situations of migration, flight, and exile, or in situations of misery unworthy of a human being in which an ordered family life is hardly possible. In our cultural ambience, industrialization has brought about the separation of dwelling, workplace, and recreational spaces and, as a result, the disintegration of the domestic community as a social unit. Many times, for professional reasons, fathers must be away from the family for long periods of time, and women who work professionally are only partially present in the family. Thus, economic conditions disturb coexistence and family cohesion.

To this is added the anthropological crisis. The modern processes of liberation and personalization in late modernity or, if you will, in "postmodernity," have led to processes of individualization that for many make it difficult, when not appearing as truly unreasonable, to enter into or maintain lasting obligations. Emancipation with respect to traditional sexual roles has brought gender theories that not only question the patterns of conventional culturally conditioned sexual roles, but the fundamental natural distinction of male and female, and that not only don't discriminate against homosexual life communities, as God wills, but propagate them as alternative life choices.[2]

The social changes that have led to the transformation and the pluralistic conception of the family place all churches before a new situation and before new challenges, because in no other ambience is so directly encountered the message of the Church and the life of the people as in that of marriage and the family. In this way the doctrine of the Church on marriage and family has modeled European family culture for many centuries; this does not mean, of course, that everyone lives by this doctrine. But until well into the first part of the twentieth century it was considered the social idea of reference that determined not only private life, but also juridical civil culture.

Without doubt, there are still families today who make every effort to live Christian faith in the family and to testify to the beauty and joy of faith lived in the bosom of the family. Meanwhile, on the other hand, for many other Christians— even practicing Christians—Church doctrine has come to appear removed from the reality of the world and life.

The Church of the first centuries was also confronted—in the Jewish context and with much greater reason the Greco-Roman—with models of marriage and family contrary to what Jesus had proclaimed. And the first disciples felt as unprecedented challenge the words of Jesus concerning the fidelity of man and woman. In this way also today, without concessions to a cheap liberal compromise, the Church must take on the challenge. Heedful of the signs of the times, she must make God's word heard anew as word of life.

THE COMMANDMENTS
AS INDICATORS OF AN UPRIGHT LIFE

The word of God is not some code of doctrines and mandates. It is the message that witnesses the way of God with mankind. The Old Testament takes as its point of departure the tradition of the ancient East of that time, which, in a long process of education in the light of faith in Yahweh, was purified and perfected step by step. That's why, in the Old Testament, are still found multiple ancient, and later surpassed, traditions. Already gathered in the second table of the Decalogue (Exod 20:12–17; Deut 5:16–21) are the results of this process of clarification and purification. In it are the fundamental values of family life under God's special protection: reverential respect for parents and care for the elderly, the inviolability of marriage, property as the basis of family life and just dealings with one another, without which no community can last.

These mandates develop the golden rule, known in all cultures in one form or another, which obliges doing unto others as you would have them do unto you, or of not doing unto others as you would not have them do unto you. The Sermon on the Mount confirms the golden rule (Matt 7:12; Luke 6:31). This rule serves as a summary of that taught by the prophets and the law (Matt 7:12; 22:40; Luke 6:31) and as natural right understood in the original sense.[3] The holy fathers were convinced that the commandments of the Decalogue coincide with the moral conscience common to all human beings.

In this way, with the Decalogue mankind has been given a kind of compass for the way that Jesus expressly confirmed (Matt 19:18ff). This compass puts in our hands the criteria by which to judge relations that contradict human dignity: polygamy, forced marriage, violence in the marriage or in the family, machismo, discrimination against the woman, prostitution, as well as unjust economic, labor, salary, and housing conditions jeopardizing the family. The Bible, therefore, does not view the commandments as a burden and as a limitation of freedom; they wish to be landmarks on the road toward a happy life. They cannot be imposed on anyone, but, with good reasons, they can be offered to everyone as the way to happiness.

THE BIBLICAL MEANING AND MODEL OF THE FAMILY

The gospel, which is always the same, is presented to us in the Bible immersed in the culture of that time, which, in its turn, was subject to great changes for immemorial ages, from the epoch of the patriarchs, ancient Israel, to early Judaism. For this reason, a concrete binding order for today cannot be deduced from singular biblical affirmations. Nevertheless, it is not without foundation that the Old Testament canon antici-pates in the first two chapters of Genesis, in somewhat pro-grammatic form, the originating plan of the creation of God. These two chapters also contain in different ways very ancient traditions of humanity that, in light of the faith in Yahweh, were critically interpreted and deepened. Hence, from them can be derived something like a binding model and meaning in which we are presented God's plan for the family.

The fundamental affirmation states, "So God created humankind in his image, in the image of God he created them; male and female he created them" (Gen 1:27). The human being, in the duality of sexes, is creation of God: good; moreover, very good. Here there is not a shred of aversion to the body or scorn for sexuality, as occurs, unfortunately, in many later ecclesial traditions. Here neither is there a place for discrimination against the woman. According to the Bible, male and female, as image of God, have the same dignity. But male and female are not simply equal. Both their equal dignity and their difference have their basis in the creation. Nobody has given it to them, nor do they give it to themselves. One doesn't become male or female by the prevalent culture. To be male and to be female have their ontological basis in the creation.

The equal dignity of their diversity is the basis for their attraction to each other, sung and celebrated by myths and the great poetry of humanity, like the Old Testament Song of Songs. Artificial ideological equality destroys erotic love. The Bible understands this love as becoming "one flesh," that is, a life community that includes sex, eros, as well as human friendship (Gen 2:24). The human being is not created by God as an isolated individual. "It is not good that the man should be alone; I will make him a helper as his partner" (2:18). That's why Adam greets the woman with an enthusiastic exclamation of welcome (2:23). Man and woman are created the one for the other and are given by God as gift of the one for the other. They must mutually complement and support each other, find pleasure and joy the one in the other. Man and woman are created for love, and in this consists being image of God, who is love (1 John 4:8).

The love between man and woman does not revolve around itself: it transcends itself and must become fecund in the children born from it (Gen 1:28). The love between man and woman and the transmission of life form a whole. This applies not only to the procreative act. The first birth is prolonged in the second birth, social and cultural, in the initiation to life and through the transmission of life values. For this, children need the protective space and the affective security of the parents' love; inversely, the children strengthen and enrich the bonds of love linking their parents.

As such, fecundity is not for the Bible just a biological reality. Children are fruit of God's blessing. God puts under the responsibility of man and woman that which is most valuable: human life. It is licit for them to decide responsibly about the number and rhythm of birth of the children. This must be done with responsibility before God and respect for the dignity and well-being of the companion, with responsibility regarding the well-being of the children, responsibility regarding the future of society, and with reverential respect for the nature of the human being. From here is deduced no casuistry, but a binding model and meaning whose concrete realization is entrusted to the responsibility of the man and the woman. To them is entrusted the responsibility for the future of humanity. Without family there is no future at all, but an aging of society—a danger for all Western societies. For the Bible, children are not burden, but wealth, joy, and blessing.

In another sense, the love between man and woman is projected outside and beyond itself. It is not a sentimentalism that revolves around itself. To them is jointly entrusted the earth (Gen 1:28). The words employed in this passage—*subdue, have dominion*—cannot be understood in the sense of violent submission and exploitation. The second narration of the creation speaks of "till[ing] and keep[ing]" (Gen 2:15), by which is signified the cultural charge to cultivate and care for the earth as a garden. Man and woman must be keepers of the world and shape it as a world worthy of the human being. This is, at the same time, a political mission; because the family, as basic and vital cell, is school of humanity and of the social virtues necessary for life and the development of society.[4] In this ordering, the family comes before the state and holds its own rights facing the latter. The rights of the family, enumerated in the Letter of the Family, have their foundation in the order of the creation.[5] The state cannot infringe upon these rights; rather, it should protect them and foment them according to its possibilities.

Finally, human love is, as image of God, something grand and beautiful, but is not in itself divine. If one member idolizes the other and expects him to provide heaven on earth, necessarily the demand is superior to his strength; in that moment, he cannot but let his companion down. Many marriages fail due to these excessive expectations. The life community of man and woman, together with their children, can be happy only if it is conceived as a gift that projects above and outside of itself. In this way the creation of the human being flows into the seventh day of creation, into the festival of the Sabbath. The Sabbath, as God's day off, should also be a day off for festival and celebration in common: a day of free time, of one with the other, of one for the other (cf. Exod 20:8–10; Deut 5:12–14). The family should be a place of festival and of celebration and of common joy, something that it continues to be today for many people.

GOD'S BLESSING AND PROMISE FOR THE FAMILY

What has been said until now constitutes an ideal picture of the family, but it is not simply the reality. The Bible also knows this. That's why, following the first two chapters of Genesis, comes the third, narrating the expulsion from the paradisiacal matrimonial reality.

Alienation, the distancing of the human being from God, has as a consequence alienation within human beings and between them. The first alienation is produced between the man and the woman. They are ashamed of each other (Gen 3:10ff). Shame demonstrates that the original harmony of body and spirit is destroyed, and that man and woman have moved apart. Attraction has degenerated into passion for each other and domination of the man over the woman (3:16). Then come violence, jealousy, and marital and familiar discord. The Bible speaks of infidelity in the couple. This infidelity penetrates even to the family tree of Jesus (Matt 1:5ff). Jesus also had ancestors who were not "well-born," which one would rather prefer to cover up and silence. The Bible is, on this point, completely realistic and honest.

The second alienation affects the women and the mothers. From now on they have to give birth to their children in stress and pain (Gen 3:16), and all too often bring them up in the midst of all kinds of troubles. How many mothers cry and sorrow for their children...! Distancing, alienation, also affects the man and his relationship with nature. The Earth is not a lovely garden; it produces thorns and thistles, it's rebellious and obstinate, work is miserable and hard. Man has to take on his work hurting and with sweat on his brow (3:19). To this is added the distancing and conflicts in the family itself: envy, fights, wars, even fratricide between brothers (Gen 4:1–6).

Finally, there is the most radical alienation: death (Gen 3:19; cf. Rom 5:12) and all the powers of death, which descend upon the world with fury wreaking misfortune, havoc, and destruction. They also bring pain and sorrow to the family—for example, when mothers mourn over the cadavers of their children, or when a member of the matrimonial couple must bid farewell to the other, often with the consequence, for people now old, of painful years of loneliness.

Biblical realism teaches that what we lament today is not exclusive to today; in essence it has always been thus. It is not licit for us to succumb to the temptation of romanticizing the past, to then consider the present as the pure history of decadence. Praise for the old days and complaints about the younger generation have existed since the existence of an older generation. Still, in the end, in the Bible hope overcomes despair. God, upon expelling the human being from paradise, has given him hope for the way: from his descendents will arise the Savior (Gen 3:15).

The Savior, according to Christian conviction, has come with Jesus Christ. He entered into a family history and grew up in the family of Nazareth (Luke 2:51ff). At the beginning of his public life he participated in the celebration of the wedding at Cana where he performed his first miracle (John 2:1–12). By this he put all of his activity under the sign of a wedding and nuptial joy. Finally, the Bible concludes with the eschatological vision of the wedding of the Lamb (Rev 19:7–9). Marriage and family are converted, in this way, into signs of eschatological hope. With the celebration of the terrestrial wedding is anticipated, so to speak, the celebration of the eschatological wedding. That's why it can and must be celebrated in all splendor and rejoicing.

We have a fundamental affirmation of Jesus about marriage and the family in his well-known sentence on divorce (Matt 19:3–9; Mark 10:2–12; Luke 16:18). Jesus refers to the originating will of God: "What God has united, man must not divide." This affirmation causes fear in the disciples. It seems to them an unheard-of attack on the idea of matrimony in the surrounding world and an unmerciful demand. "If that is the condition of the husband with the wife, better not to marry." Jesus indirectly confirms the novelty of the demand. This unconditional faithfulness has to be "given" to the human being; it is a gift of grace. It supposes the transformation of hardheartedness (Matt 19:8) into a new, compassionate heart, as promised by the prophet (Ezek 36:26ff).

Therefore it is not licit to interpret the word of Jesus as inflexible law. This is also demonstrated by the diverse interpretations of these words in the Judeo-Christian and Christian-pagan contexts respectively. They must be understood in the integral context of Jesus' message about the kingdom of God as a message of grace, love, and compassion.[6] The alliance established by the married couple is sealed and supported by the alliance of God. God's promise of alliance and fidelity removes the human alliance from human arbitrariness, conferring upon it stability and consistency. It is strength and a constant source of energy, amidst the vicissitudes of life, for maintaining mutual fidelity.

Paul echoes the message of Jesus and speaks of a marriage "in the Lord." This "in the Lord" embraces, as shown in the "domestic tables" (Col 3:18—4:1; Eph 5:21—6:9; 1 Pet 2:18—3:7), the entire life of the family, the relations of husband and wife, parents and children, freemen and slaves who live in the house. The domestic tables assume the patriarchal domestic order of that time; notwithstanding, "in the Lord" converts the unilateral submission of the woman to the man into a mutual relationship of love that must also impregnate the rest of family relations. These are examples of the force of the Christian faith to modify and create norms.

The Letter to the Ephesians goes a step further. It assumes the Old Testament metaphor of the matrimonial alliance as characterization of the alliance of God with his people. In Christ that alliance has found its realization and consummation. In this way, the alliance of man and woman is now converted into a real symbol of the alliance of God with human beings that has reached its fulfillment in Christ Jesus. What from the beginning was a reality of the "good" creation of God is now converted into sign of the presence of the mystery of Christ and of the Church (Eph 5:32). The Council of Trent saw in this affirmation the sacramentality of matrimony.[7] Recent theology seeks to deepen this christological basis in its trinitarian aspect and to understand the family as a symbolic-real representation of the mystery of the trinitarian community of Father, Son, and Holy Spirit.

The idea of marriage-sacrament is the basis of a difference from the idea of matrimony of the Protestant churches. However, the coincidence is greater than the difference, because, even though matrimony, from a Protestant perspective, is a civil state, the celebration of marriage is united to an ecclesial act of benediction. It is defined as a divine and sacred state.[8] Only juridically is matrimony a civil matter, under the competence of the civil authority, not ecclesiastical. This, in a society impregnated with Christianity, might be feasible, but in a secularized society, opposed to the original intention, it leads to spiritually problematic adaptations. The civil and spiritual spheres are not differentiated but jumbled, and in practice there is an accented secularization of marriage.. The introduction by the Council of Trent[9] of a canonical form proper to the celebration of matrimony has proven, on the contrary, to be the most far-seeing initiative, most apt to conserve and protect the spiritual dimension of marriage.

As sacrament, matrimony is not a static magnitude. It needs, like the Church herself, continuous renewal, both juridically and spiritually. The juridical norms have to be continuously examined to see if and how they can conserve and protect pastorally, in the best manner possible, the spiritual essence. Spiritually, all marriage is under the law of process and gradualism, of growth continually renewed and deepened in the mystery of Christ (*Familiaris consortio* 9; 34). It must continually travel the way of conversion, renewal, and maturation. Tolerance, forgiveness, and patience must be exercised over and over: to always reserve time for one another, demonstrations of affection, esteem, tenderness, gratitude, and love are constantly necessary. It is important to celebrate festivals together. Prayer, the sacrament of confession, and the celebration of the Eucharist in common are always aids for consolidating and renewing the bond of marriage. It is touching to meet with elderly couples who, in spite of their advanced years, are in love in a mature way. This is a sign of saved human life, humanly and spiritually mature.

LOOKING TO THE FUTURE:
THE FAMILY AS DOMESTIC CHURCH

Not only are the individual couples and families on the way. The Church also has already traveled in modern history a way toward the comprehension of marriage and the family, and has to retravel it today with married couples and families. In this context, we can't go deeper into said history and its multiple vicissitudes. We're only going to make a reference to a change of tendency signified by the Vatican II. In the late Middle Ages, the Church appropriated, with some modifications, the idea of matrimony of Roman law and viewed marriage as a contract realized by means of the consent of the parties. This contractual idea has determined the thought of the modern age and civil matrimonial law.

The Second Vatican Council signified a reorientation. It understood marriage as a community of life and love, and the wedding as a covenant in which the bride and groom give themselves to and receive each other mutually (Pastoral Constitution on the Church in the Modern World, *Gaudium et spes* 48). More recent ecclesiastical declarations have further developed this biblical personalist perspective.[10] Postcouncil canonic law has assimilated it, but many singular dispositions have remained bound to inherited theory.[11] A subsequent discussion, clarification, and reform is needed, then.

The discussion has focused, mainly, on the problem of those who divorce and remarry. This is, without doubt, a pressing pastoral problem about which entire libraries have already been written and into which here we are not going to enter anew.[12] In truth, it would be a fatal lack of insight to consider the question of admittance to the sacraments of the divorced and remarried as an isolated problem. This problem is part of an entire pastoral renewal concerning marriage and family. Already at the beginning it was made clear that there are many other—and essentially more fundamental—problems that are still under discussion and await an adequate answer.

It is of overriding importance that the Church regain, in questions of sexuality, marriage, and family, the capacity for communication and not emerge from the stagnation in resigned silence or a purely defensive posture in face of the present situation. The fundamental problem is how the Church can pastorally help people to find happiness and fulfillment in life. Part of this is formed by the responsible and gratifying use of the gift of sexuality, bequeathed and entrusted by the Creator to the human being. Sexuality must leave behind the narrowness and solitude of a self-centered individualism and set its course for the *You* of the other person as well as the *Us* of the human community. To isolate sexuality from such relationships and bonds of universal human dimension, reducing it to sex alone, has led not to its much-vaunted freedom, but to banality and commercialization. The death of erotic love and the senescence of our Western society are the results. Marriage and family are the last nest of resistance against a coldly calculating economism and technification of life that engorges all. Therefore, we are in the right to commit ourselves, according to our strength, in favor of marriage and family and, above all, to accompany and encourage young people on this path.

With good words alone little can be achieved. In light of worsening conditions, both economic and moral-spiritual, for marriage and family, it is necessary to offer specific paths. Christ has already shown us the direction of this way. He says no Christian, married or single, abandoned by their partner or educated in childhood or youth without contact with their own family, is ever alone or lost. They have a home in a new family of brothers and sisters (Matt 12:48–50; 19:27–29). Here are laid the foundations of the community of disciples and, with it, of the Church as new family, and of the family as domestic church.

In antiquity, together with the father of the family and his wife and children, relatives, slaves, and sometimes also friends or guests often formed part of the household. In this context we should understand that when the primitive community is spoken of, the first Christians met in the houses (Acts 2:26; 5:42). The conversion of entire households is constantly mentioned (Acts 11:14; 16:15, 31:33). In Paul, the Church was organized by houses, that is, by domestic churches (Rom 16:5; 1 Cor 16:19; Col 4:15; Phlm 2). The houses were for Paul support and starting points for his missionary journeys; they were centers of foundation and pillars of the local communities; they were places of prayer, catechetical teaching, Christian fraternity, and hospitality for traveling Christians. In this way, the Church in the domestic churches was to be a house open to all; in it everyone was to feel at home and in family.

In subsequent history, the domestic churches have always played an important role. Above all in situations of minority, diaspora, or persecution, they became for the Church a question of life and death. The Second Vatican Council newly takes up the idea. Its few citations have become, in postcouncil documents, in-depth chapters.[13] In Latin America, Africa, Asia (Philippines, India, Korea, among others), domestic churches in the form of *basic Christian communities* or *small Christian communities* have turned out to be a formula for pastoral success.[14]

In Western civilization, where longtime popular ecclesial structures prove less and less consistent, pastoral spaces become larger, and Christians frequently find themselves in the cultural minority, the domestic churches can be converted into foundation stones of a Church with possibilities for the future. It's obvious that today we cannot simply reproduce the domestic churches of the primitive Church. We need a new brand of extended families. For small families to survive in the present situation, they have to be inserted into a family structure that spans generations, where the grandparents play an especially important role; into interfamilial circles of neighbors and friends where the children, in their parents' absence, are looked after and where elderly people living alone, divorced persons, and all those learning on their own can find a certain family atmosphere. Apostolic and religious communities are frequently the space and environment for familial communities. Other initiatives for the formation of domestic churches are found in prayer and Bible study groups, in catechisms, ecumenical encounters, and others.

The domestic churches are *ecclesiola in ecclesia*, churches in miniature within the greater Church. They make the Church present in the midst of life, because where two or three are gathered in the name of Christ, he is there among them (Matt 18:20). By virtue of baptism and confirmation, the domestic communities are the messianic people of God. They participate in the priestly, prophetic, and royal ministry (1 Pet 2:8; cf. Rev 1:6; 5:10). Thanks to the Holy Spirit, they possess the *sensus fidei*, the sense of the faith, a sixth, intuitive sense for faith and for a life praxis fitted to the gospel. Thus, they are not only the object, but the subject of family pastoral action. Above all, with their example, they can help the Church to penetrate more deeply in the word of God and to apply it more fully in life (Francis, Apostolic Letter *Evangelii gaudium*). Since the Holy Spirit has been given to the Church as a whole, they cannot isolate themselves, like a sect, from the greater *communio* of the Church. This "catholic principle" protects the Church from disintegration into free, singular, and autonomic churches. Through such unity in plurality, the Church is truly a sacramental sign of unity in the world.

Concretely, the domestic churches, sharing the Bible, draw from the word of God light and strength for daily life. In view of the rupture in the transmission of faith to the next generation, they have the important catechetical task of bringing children, young people, and adults to the joy of faith.[15] In their personal desires and in the desires of the world, they pray together. The Sunday Eucharist must be jointly celebrated with the entire community, as source and summit of all Christian life. In the family circle they celebrate the Lord's Day as a day of leisure, happiness, and community, and they observe the distinct moments of the liturgical year in the wealth of their traditions and customs. They are spaces of spirituality in the community where each receives the other in the spirit of love, forgiveness, and reconciliation; where, every day, Sundays, and feast days, joys and sorrows, worries, needs and mourning, joy and human happiness are shared.

The families, as domestic churches, are called in a special way to transmit the faith in their respective surroundings. Theirs is a personal, prophetic mission. Their testimony is, principally, the testimony of life, by which they can act in the world as leaven (Matt 13:33). As Christ has come to announce the good news to the poor and suffering, to the little ones and the children (Matt 5:3ff; 11:25; Luke 6:20ff), likewise, he has sent his disciples to announce the gospel to the poor (Luke 7:22). Therefore, it is not licit for the domestic Churches to be elitist and exclusive. They have to open themselves to those who suffer need of any kind, to the simple and the humble. They must know that the kingdom of God belongs to the children (Mark 10:14; cf. *EG* 197–201).

The families need the Church and the Church needs the families to be present in the midst of life and in the spheres of modern society. Without the domestic churches, the Church is removed from the concrete reality of life. Only through the families can the Church be a domestic church where people are at home. The idea of the Church as domestic church is, for this reason, fundamental for the future of the Church and for the new evangelization. The families are the first and best messengers of the gospel of the family. They are the way of the Church toward the future.

6

"DO NOT HIDE YOURSELF FROM YOUR OWN KIN"

Reflections from the Perspective of the Catholic Church on the Fundamental Importance of the Family

REINHARD MARX

&

"Is it not to share your bread with the hungry, and bring the homeless poor into your house; when you see the naked, to cover them, and not to hide yourself from your own kin? Then your light shall break forth like the dawn, and your healing shall spring up quickly" (Isa 58:7–8). A citation from the prophet Isaiah: and there, in the middle of the moral exhortations to be better people and to construct a better society, we read, "Do not hide yourself from your own kin!" This is also family from the biblical viewpoint—maybe something different from that which we are used to. Here is not stalwartly sung an ardent hymn to the family, or is its beauty lauded. Made palpable is an experience that also belongs to the family: the family is trying, a burden that perhaps one would gladly be got rid of. Most likely, all of us know such family situations, in which one could get by perfectly well without the "dear relatives," and in which the community of destiny that is the family turns out to be more destiny than community. But without wavering against the background of such experiences the prophet sticks to his guns: "Do not turn away from your kin! Then your light shall break forth like the dawn." So then, to look out for the family and the relatives has intrinsic value, a value that is encountered beyond the momentary sensation of well-being and immediate personal interest. There is room to object, of course, that the prophet directed these words to a considerably premodern society, in which insertion in the family and the clan still had an importance very different from ours in relation to the well-being and even the survival of the person. Who is not content to freely translate the prophet's exhortation, for example, as "Do something for your family!"? But, beyond the opinion that this exhortation is still valid today, its manner of justification must be explained. What role does the family play in the society of the twenty-first century? What does it mean for the individual, for the society as a whole, and also for the Church? And finally, why does it continue to be right today not to wash one's hands of service to the family? We will deal with this in what follows. But before occupying ourselves with these questions, it would be good to make some observations concerning the manner in which here we will look at the family and about what concept of the family is pre-supposed as a consequence.

WHAT "LOOK" AT THE FAMILY?

The family is never abstract but always concrete. When the family is spoken of, each brings with him his own completely concrete experiences as a background of comprehension. This must be kept in mind when the theme of family is taken up. Otherwise, right away the impression arises that what is said overlooks the vital reality of the family and is nothing more than an accumulation of bad personal experiences or idealistic phrases. But, on the other hand, it is not enough to describe, however rigorously, from the standpoint of the social sciences, what goes on in present daily life without taking a look at what the family can or even should be. Reflections on the family cannot, therefore, be limited to a descriptive perspective; they must also adopt a normative-prescriptive perspective. This must be done in permanent reference to the descriptive perspective, but still needs to be unequivocally designated as normative. Otherwise, the normative ideas creep in, so to speak, uninvited, and therefore without reflection, if only in the sense of "the way things are is the way they should be." But with the way things are, the prophet cited at the beginning of these considerations could not be satisfied, as neither can be satisfied any other person who desires growth and development for the better. So then, the look at the family will be multidimensional only when both the descriptive aspect— "what the family is specifically"—and the normative perspective—"what the family can be"—are incorporated. At this point one would have to ask critically, Then where does this normative-prescriptive perspective come from? In this respect, little echo will be found for arguments limited to a reference without further explanation to the "meaning of the family from the point of view of natural law" or to the "essence of the family." The question as to whether an iusnaturalistic foundational model has meaning—and if so, what—would require a specific debate that we cannot take up here. But from the standpoint of "human ecology" (Pope Benedict XVI), a perspective very near to natural law has recently acquired new standing.

Here we will confine ourselves to a discussion starting from longstanding empirical values that together form an ideal of marriage and family, and that provide us with information about life conditions favorable to the success of the couple and to paternity and maternity. In the exegesis of Sacred Scripture and in her tradition, the Church conserves such longstanding empirical values and offers them to the people of today as critical counterpoint to the concrete experiences of marriage and family. This ideal also has relevance beyond the circle of pious Catholics, inasmuch as it wishes to counsel all those in search of a good life. In the perspective of the society as a whole, it represents a contribution to the normative argument, which, while unable to possess a binding character for everyone, prudence bids us to evaluate and keep in mind. Last, it's a good idea not to simply set aside without further ado that which has been accredited, but to ponder whether it might not be recommendable or even necessary to conserve it, so as to foment social development instead of uprooting it. But neither is it wise to cling to tradition reflexively or from mere conservatism; nor is the latest social fashion always immediately and automatically the most propitious for the future and that which opens the most new perspectives. In this sense, the present challenges facing the family must be taken seriously, and lines of solution sought in keeping with the times, but this without neglecting the critical perspective of the present associated with historically shaped ideals. From here it must also be asked whether modern society and the family shouldn't adapt to their already accredited fundamental structures, rather than it having to be always the other way around.

WHAT MODEL OF FAMILY?

First, it should be somewhat further explained, transcending the definition of *family founded on matrimony*, what was earlier alluded to by the term *ideal*. The point of departure of this notion is the idea that sexuality is counted among the fundamental dimensions—the so-called existential ones—of the human being. Consequently, it affects not only the corporal-biological side, but also always has something to do with the person. But since man is a relational being, a being that needs others in order to exist, sexuality is also associated with the aspect of personal relation. Sexuality is thus always subject to the demand to be symbol, expression, and means of a personal relationship of love between a *you* and a *me*. Willingness, equality of rights, exclusivity, and mutual respect for the dignity of the person are, therefore, inseparably linked with this aspiration. If sexuality is not up to the demand of being expression of true love, the "fall into intranscendence" (P. Ricoeur) is inevitable. The love between man and woman always takes place in tense relation between erotic desire and affectionate and solicitous caring. Pleasure, affectionate closeness, and fecundity, satisfaction with the other, and the generation of new life, here jointly have their place in life. In this, love is not depleted in the magic of the instant, but asks spontaneously to last. An "I love you" that springs from the heart does not commiserate, ultimately, with any temporal limitation. It establishes indefectibly the arch between "fidelity and betrayal" (G. Marcel). The lovers, once they have said, "I love you" for the first time, cannot but confront this tension. Hence love also needs the promise, the firm guarantee: "I will stand by you." The solemn formulation of this guarantee before God and men takes place in the nuptial celebration. In it, the lovers say to each other, not in secret but loud and clear, that they want to hold to their love for better or worse, in sickness and health, until death do them part. The alliance that this promise seals as alliance for life is situated at the intersection between the private intimacy of the couple's love life, on one side, and social-institutional integration, on the other. That's why this highly personal and intimate relationship is simultaneously recognized, protected, and fomented with all juridical-official formality. The official community owes this respect to matrimony since marriage is not founded by the state, but precedes it.

The Christian ideal starts from the premise that it is good for people to freely commit themselves and jointly propose a high and ambitious goal; but at the same time it starts from the premise that this alliance creates the most appropriate protected environment for the birth and bringing up of children. There where the lovers, as spouses, promise faithfulness, and fulfill this promise with all sincerity of heart, the primordial confidence (*Urvertrauen*) of the children can also take root, and the responsibility for their upbringing can be shared.

But an important aspect of this ideal is the dynamic of personal development. According to this, neither is marriage reduced to the moment of the nuptials, nor are marriage and family understood as something static. Hence, it is not sufficient to marry, start a family and just go with the flow. It's a matter of ceaseless commitment to the cultivation of the couple's conjugal relationship, but also to the rest of the familial relations. Again the words of the prophet resound in our ears: "Do not hide yourself from your own kin!" However, it goes without saying that we all also make mistakes regarding marriage and family, that things go awry and lead where they shouldn't, that we treat each other badly. That's why it's so important to continually reach out to meet each other, to seek pathways of communication, to critically question ourselves. But an ideal serves precisely for this. It's also indispensable to forgive each other, to allow new beginnings, to perceive how others are developing, giving them space while at the same time remaining spiritually close and in communication.

The aim is to develop together and mature thanks to the relationship with the other. No doubt, this is a high ideal regarding which many would not hesitate to say that it's too good to be true or even impossible to put into practice. Why then does the Church embrace it with such insistence? Is it not a case of an elaborate negation of reality? Against this must be set the already cited thesis that it is good for the human being to make an effort for marriage and family. But this has to be explained both in respect to the individual and to the society as a whole.

MARRIAGE AND FAMILY
FOR THE INDIVIDUAL

In premodern times, no one asked if it was good for the individual to live in a family. For most people it was necessary for survival, if only for the reason that the individual wasn't in a position to support an *oîkos*, a home that could function adequately. In any case, one could substitute for the family community other forms of community, such as, for example, monastic life. Although these were more extended than at present, they were still special forms, whereas the norm was life in the family consort. Only modern society, with an elevated division of labor, makes it possible for numerous people to live alone and keep up a one-person home. Apart from the diverse motives that lead people to live alone, single people also have, in any case, a family of origin. In their family of origin, people are born, grow, know for the first time the fundamental experiences of acceptance, establish bonds and, from that security, become able to go out into the surroundings, assimilate new impressions, and feel the world as their own. For a newborn, the family signifies almost everything, and only very slowly, step by step, do children loosen attachments to the bosom of the family of origin. When the family is lacking, it is very difficult to find a substitute for the children. But when a family functions, be it only to a certain extent, its contribution goes much beyond—immeasurably beyond—mere physical care: from solicitous affection to inculcating religion and culture, from education to fomenting emotional and cognitive capacities. For the child, the family is an infinite, first rate "source," and continues to be so later for the adult. In a way, the entire system of social services existing in modern European societies can be considered as a result of the effort to compensate for, or at least attenuate, the imponderable lack of family bonds. This is an achievement that is to be greatly valued and that contributes in an essential way to the humanization of society. We must be aware, however, that this is, in fact, only the mitigation of a want and that, seen as a whole, life without family bonds does not, by a long shot, constitute a better alternative. We must stick with the idea that the importance of the family for the individual is self-evident and has a value difficult to overestimate. All those who have been bequeathed a loving family of origin are to be grateful!

Considerably less evident is the importance of founding one's own family. If the family of origin is so important, then—it could be thought—it should likewise be the most natural thing in the world to transmit this inestimable good to the next generation. We experience today in a very peculiar way that this is not something automatic. We have the seemingly paradoxical situation that today an overwhelming majority of young people wish to found, sooner or later, their own family, but for a large number of them this wish is not fulfilled in subsequent years in the manner that they would have liked. The reasons for this development are much debated and it appears that it is a consequence of a web of quite unmanageable factors. The duration and complexity of education, the commencement of professional life, and economic and social consolidation play here, undoubtedly, a relevant role, as do the far from clear perspectives concerning the reconciliation of work and family life, especially for women, the high expectations concerning the quality of family life, the uncertainty about one's own future, and the difficulty to decide when is the right moment to start a family. There is also now the problem of finding the adequate companion for a future in common. Likely even more reasons could be mentioned. The upshot is that numerous people cannot see fulfilled a wish that would represent a great opportunity in their lives. The experiences that a person has upon becoming a parent are not existentially indispensable. If they were, it would imply that all those who don't have this good fortune could not, in the last analysis, find meaning in their life. Nevertheless, such experiences are significant, existentially moving, and profoundly transformative for life. They foment the awareness of responsibility, make manifest the meaning of life, and destroy supposed, often overly oppressive, notions of order. Of course, they also cost effort, vital force, and nerves. Above all, they proffer the profound impression of the meaning of life as a daily new gift. But a fulfilled relationship with adult sons and daughters also represents an inestimable enrichment of life. In an epoch in which life expectancy has grown enormously, the specificity of the relation between grandparents and grandchildren has likewise been rediscovered. The familial coexistence of the generations contains vital treasures that beg to be conserved. Clearly, everything here doesn't always work out well; mistakes are also made in this terrain and limits reached. But not to take advantage of this life opportunity supposes already beforehand an important renunciation that should be well thought through and weighed. Whoever blithely rules out this possibility is doing himself, or herself, a disservice. An important task profiled against this background is to encourage young adults to found their own family and to shape the framework of society in such a way that they can really dare to do so without the fear of ending up as losers, disfavored, or outsiders. A society that makes it difficult for young adults to start their own families, to be mothers and fathers, is negating for them a vital perspective of capital importance.

Even less evident than the importance of the family for the individual is the importance of marriage for him or her. Why is it good to link life as a couple and in paternity and maternity to this traditional institution, weighed down by middle-class mediocrity and threatened to a large degree with failure? These reflections on the ideal have already anticipated what can be said in this respect. Valid here is also that which was previously affirmed: insofar as it is a vital institution of support, marriage has lost its importance. Today nobody needs to get married in order to assure existence or to maintain social position. But neither is this, in reality, the core meaning of marriage, and therefore this aspect turns out to be, in fact, dispensable. What is it, then, that makes matrimony still attractive? Matrimony fits with a love lived seriously and can strengthen it decisively and long-lastingly. In marriage, the lovers promise mutually not to neglect this love, but to nourish its ardor, to the end that the flame between them is not extinguished. They do this speaking clearly and out loud, thus laying out a path of reliability, both for the other and for themselves, in the midst of a world of insecurities and always more accelerated change. Immersed in a network of biographical transformations heretofore unimaginable, they weave a common guideline. With this they establish at the same time a solid alliance that opens the protecting and accepting space where the vital spheres of sexuality, fecundity, and paternity and maternity can be experienced; it is delicate and vulnerable and, for this very reason, in need of protection.

Marriage in a Christian perspective has, finally, one more, all-determining aspect. In matrimony, love is situated also—and not least of all—in the horizon of God. This is not a pious afterthought, but expresses existential relevance. Precisely due to such a lofty relational ethic, the danger of a notorious excess of self-demand may easily appear, and more so if the relationship is wreathed in an aura of romanticism. Whoever intends to offer heaven on earth to the loved one, and expects in return the satisfaction of all longings and hopes, fails inevitably because of the hard realities. Neither repeated attempts with new partners nor the cynical negation of the human being's innate capacity to love offer any real way out of this situation. Alleviating and useful, conversely, is the fundamental attitude of faith, which does everything humanly possible, but hopes in God for salvation and ultimate fulfillment. This fundamental attitude is expressed concretely in the Catholic conception of marriage as sacrament, as effective sign of divine love.

It's not a question of talking up marriage as if it were an "unsellable article." But in these brief allusions the great potential of matrimony can already be recognized, and how worthwhile it is to reflect seriously on the adventure of marriage instead of rushing to reject it.

MARRIAGE AND FAMILY FOR THE SOCIETY

With marriage and family society as a whole gains at least as much as individuals do. This gain that society draws from the family starts with biological reproduction, without which the succession of generations would not exist, but it doesn't stop there by any means. Families not only give birth to future "people useful for society," but additionally raise, educate, form, and accompany them on their way toward life. Other institutions of accompaniment, education, and formation cannot, in this respect, but play a complementary role and build on the foundations laid by the family. Where family is lacking, society must make a considerable effort in order to compensate this absence. The attempts to make the family dispensable for society in this sense have never been successful in the history of humanity. Of course, to decide how much is to be left to the families in this terrain, and how much society claims for itself is a weighty question. External circumstances, objective constrictions, and set mentalities and customs play an important role in this. The aspect of justice of opportunities will always be a key reason here for not leaving the family to face this task alone. A society in which young peoples' future opportunities depend solely on the family of origin generates great inequalities. But those who think, on the other hand, that the state can do all that a family does much better and more professionally are fooling themselves regarding the importance of the family, and overburden state institutions and actions with excessive demands. State intervention in the family sphere always has the character of a measure of urgency, and state action in this sphere is never but an attempt to handle something with inadequate instruments. The only reasonable perspective that opens up is to reflect and act in common. Most important has to be to foment, back, and complement families in the tasks that are their own, to keep them in contact with other families as well as with formative institutions. Instead of replacing families, it's a matter of procuring as far as possible their ability to develop well as primary educative and formative institutions and for their potential and resources to be taken advantage of. Here there is no place for a custodial politics intending to impose the most rigid control and to direct families in the most precise manner to a concrete ideal of the configuration of family life. In their daily life families have to juggle countless demands, expectations, needs, constrictions, urgencies, and desires. In order to manage this they need a certain room to maneuver to take on a given situation in one way or another. If everything is stipulated beforehand, the family quickly goes off course.

But the family's relevance from a social viewpoint is far from being limited to its role as institution of "reproduction, education, and formation." Earlier it was emphasized that the family continues to be important also for adults. The equivalent idea from the social perspective is that, being at the same time microstructure and social glue, the family turns out to be indispensable. The notion that a society can be formed by highly mobile and flexible individuals who provisionally couple, like at a space station, here, there, or wherever, only to soon move on elsewhere, is false through and through. People need to bond, which explains why, in just such a highly complex, mobile, and flexible society as ours, the importance of counterweights to these centrifugal forces increases in a special way. Precisely when much of society is in flux, the family, as anchor and stable path of integration for individuals, becomes extremely important to guarantee global stability and to favor the further positive development of our society. In this sense, it must be noticed—and taken into consideration—that the family, despite its weight and dynamism, does not oppose—nor create obstacles for—a social change for the better; rather, it reinforces it and gives it durability.

From this angle, a look at the social relevance of marriage is also appropriate. On occasion, it seems as if both society and the state should maintain a neutral position regarding marriage, so as not to unduly limit the free decision of the individual. Marriage is then gladly considered as a private matter that, therefore, should not have fiscal consequences. Otherwise, it is argued, other styles of life would be jeopardized and discriminated. Can it really not matter to society whether or not its members make decisions of such profound individual consequences as marriage? Concerning the stability of microsocial bonds in a society, clearly a very considerable importance corresponds to matrimony. That two people bond, assume responsibility for one another, give mutual support, are disposed to procreate, and, moreover, promise all of this firmly and solemnly by all that is sacred to them, cannot but be considered beneficial for the positive development of a society. So then, truly there are good reasons to promote matrimony, reasons that have nothing at all to do with mere clinging to traditional conventions. In this sense, marriage is too often undervalued. Its central role in society becomes evident only by considering what marriage and family accomplish in the care of spouses, parents, and other family members. Also in this sphere, the overburdening of social and state institutions would be inevitable if it were wished to replace or redefine marriage and family.

MARRIAGE AND FAMILY
FOR THE CHURCH

The relevance of marriage and family for the Church deserves special consideration in this context. Attention has already been directed to the privileged condition of the family as environment of transmission of the faith. However, the first religious impressions that the children receive in the family cannot be reduced to the intellective, as if it were a catechetical instruction. The family is the ambience in which the child develops primordial confidence (*Urvertrauen*), has his first and fundamental shaping experiences, formulates his first questions about the meaning of life; and as a general rule, the family continues to be the lifelong ambience of unlimited acceptance and personal bonds. Furthermore, the family is the ambience in which the praxis of the faith and daily religious rituals are observed, such as, for example, prayer and blessing. In it the Christian festivals are celebrated, even after infancy. Questions that arise from experiences associated with sickness, suffering, death, and mourning have a key place in the family. Thus, a plethora of relations exist between family and religion, which makes of the family a prime interlocutor for the Church. In this perspective, faith unfolds in the intersection of family and Church.

However, when it's necessary to speak of religious matters, parents today often feel out of their depth. They would like to offer to their children, who are growing up in a complex and plural society, fundamental orientations for the way, but quite frequently they themselves feel insecure in the terrain of religious orientation, so that they are usually close-mouthed about it or trust that this aspect of education will be assumed more intensely by institutions that support the family, like day care and schools, as well as the parish. In this respect, a deeper dialogue with parents is to be desired, one that explores how the potentials of the family can be integrated here.

Clearly, these general reflections on family and Church are completed and deepened once again when the relation between marriage and Church is considered. For the Catholic Church, marriage is a sacrament. This means, on one hand, that she grants to matrimony a special theological rank, and believes and testifies that in matrimony divine grace becomes present in an effective way. But on the other hand, it also means that the Church knows herself to be profoundly associated with marriage. Christian spouses live in mutual caring bond that which constitutes the charge and life of the Church as a whole: to be sign of the loving presence of God among human beings. Where a Christian marriage strives to achieve harmonious relations; where the spouses, passing through the turbulences of life, meet each other ceaselessly with love and affection; there not only do they irradiate as a couple something profoundly encouraging from a human point of view, but the Church, the entire community of believers, to which they belong and in which they are integrated, also becomes a bit more "salt of the earth" and "city on the hilltop" whose light does not remain hidden. Here is made patent what it means that the sacraments are the vital realizations of the Church. It's obvious that the Church, for this reason, holds a very special relationship with marriage. For her it must be a fundamental objective that matrimony be protected, cared for, honored, but above all lived. Still and all, success is not assured beforehand for Christian sacramental matrimony. All the more important, then, must it be for the Church to defend structural positions that favor this success.

For the Church, marriage and family are not arbitrary social structures. Nor are they customs of which she has become fond and from which it is difficult for her to separate. They are part of the Church and at the same time an indispensable counterpoint to her. In a way, they belong to the *depositum fidei*, to the deposit of faith.

PERSPECTIVES

In this kind of panoramic reflection—which, consequently, has often had to keep to a general plane—it has been shown unequivocally that marriage and family have a capital importance both for the individual and for the society as a whole. At least two fundamental consequences derived from these affirmations should be mentioned here.

Such elevated and irrevocable goods as family and marriage deserve all of our efforts for the sake of their protection and promotion. The problems, critical aspects, threats, and difficulties that marriage and family experience in the societies of the twenty-first century are numerous and mentioned so frequently in debate that it is not necessary to repeat them here. However, in view of the sustaining functions of marriage and family in the building of human coexistence, the solution to these problems cannot consist in the search for other, entirely distinct structures. It was not too long ago that in numerous social science publications, the death of the family was spoken of—too hastily, as was later demonstrated. To declare today marriage a discontinued model is, at least, equally hasty. Also—and especially—in view of the problems and phenomena of crisis that surround marriage and family, what is needed is rather a process of reflection of the whole society on what can be done in the long term on multiple planes with an eye to favoring the stabilization of marriage and family. In this it must be especially kept in mind that marriage and family are considered de facto as autonomous realities with their own dynamic and their own vital realizations. The fact that marriage and family contribute so much to society not infrequently induces other social actors to select the contributions of the family useful to them and attempt to manipulate the family under this aspect. But, like it or not, the family doesn't exist solely as labor mediator for the work market, as consumer with augmented needs, or as free time compensation for stressed workers. What is necessary, rather, is a sincere debate about what it is that families themselves really need, and it is evident that such a debate cannot take place apart from the families themselves.

But the second consequence gleaned from the preceding reflections is this: to the extent that to the family and also to marriage corresponds this special relevance that we have just outlined, the announcements of crisis, the funeral dirges, and, above all, the apocalyptic scenarios of decadence are too near-sighted and pessimistic, because they don't keep in mind to what point people long for just that which marriage and family, when they function well, offer. This does not mean, of course, that it is possible to close our eyes to the problems, or that marriage and family can tranquilly be abandoned to their fate. Spouses and families need recognition and energetic backing. But from the family there is still room to expect, without doubt, something of resistance, longevity, and capacity for adaptation to transformed social realities. For this reason, marriage and family conserve essentially their importance. Upon such confidence it is possible to continue building as long as we support and strengthen the families.

7

THE HOLY FAMILY

Model for the Family as Domestic Church

KURT KOCH

∽

At Christmastime, between the feast of the birth of Jesus and that of Holy Mary, Mother of God, the feast of the Holy Family, the first of the year, is celebrated in the Catholic Church. This feast was introduced principally in the seventeenth century, was extended with force in the nineteenth, in 1921 was included in the liturgical calendar, and, with the liturgical reform following the Vatican II, was situated on the Sunday between Christmas and New Year's Day.

This liturgical placement in the life of the Church expresses a central dimension of the mystery of Christmas: that Christ, the only begotten Son of God, has become man not in an abstract sense, but in a totally concrete form, as son of a human family. In Luke's infancy narrative, this dimension is highlighted by the fact that the shepherds, first witnesses of the birth of Jesus, found the newborn Jesus not alone in the stable of Bethlehem, but together with his mother and father. "So they went with haste and found Mary and Joseph, and the child lying in the manger" (Luke 2:16). Paul expressed the same dimension with insuperable concision: "But when the fullness of time had come, God sent his Son, born of a woman, born under the law" (Gal 4:4). The Son of God wished to become man in such a concrete form that he decided to be born and grow up in a human family. God himself born in him, in the bosom of a family, was how he wished to reveal himself to men, so that Jesus Christ's belonging to a human family forms a permanent part of the substance of the incarnation. By the fact that the Son of God was born in the bosom of a human family, the Holy Family became the model of the human family, and an icon of God himself, above all in the mystery of the trinitarian God.[1] This fact raises the question of the importance of the Holy Family for the life of the Christian family today and of its message for the family in general.

THE QUESTION OF THE FAMILY AS A QUESTION OF THE HUMAN BEING

When Pope Benedict XV, in the year 1921, included the feast of the Holy Family in the liturgical calendar of the Church, he wanted to situate in plain sight, in the crisis that the family was then going through, a "marvelous example," as is expressed in the prayer of this feast day. This definition of the meaning of the festival has lost none of its relevance in the present situation, in which the crisis of family has become even more radical and manifest. Already, Vatican II, in its Pastoral Constitution on the Church and the Modern World, *Gaudium et spes*, wherein the problems, then current and pressing, of the people and the human community are taken up, dedicated its attention in the first place to "promote the dignity of marriage and the family" (*Gaudium et spes* 47–52).

In this fact can be perceived "a prophetic inspiration in view of the great difficulties which have weighed upon the familial institution in recent times."[2] This principal challenge, which forms part of the permanent legacy of Vatican II, has, in the meantime, become ever more dramatic, such that today the familiar institution is subject to multiple questions, ranging from its undervaluation in the public discourse of the society, to the disdain for its identity and rights, to the conscious and juridically legitimated identification of other forms of human coexistence with the family in its human and Christian sense.

Given that, according to the Christian conception, the familial institution is based on the institution of matrimony between a man and a woman, which is sealed for the entire life and that is characterized by fidelity and indissolubility, the present crisis of marriage and family must be tackled from its roots. The most profound problem must be seen, without a shadow of doubt, in the growing and extended incapacity of people to make binding and definitive decisions, an incapacity intimately related to the situation of modern mentality. The historical sciences have demonstrated the constant change of all things human and the rejection of the idea of permanence. The human sciences, especially psychology and sociology, incite people to ignore the definitive and to consider human life as a continuous stream of decisions, one after another. The theory of evolution fully dilutes the stability of the world into repetitive processes, and considers the human being purely and simply as a stage in the history of becoming. In this situation of modern mentality, which Pope Francis qualifies insightfully as the "culture of the provisional," binding decisions and faithfulness hardly figure anymore among the primary values, because more and more people have become as recalcitrant to relationships as they are avid to have them. This attitude can be recognized in how rare it is nowadays to refer to "my spouse"; it is preferred to speak of "my partner" or "my current partner." With this is posed, with pointed awareness, the decisive question for the health of the person and the well-being of the human community: What kind of person answers to the definition of human being? Is it the playboy who flits from one fleeting encounter to another and in this whirl has no time at all to really establish a relationship with a concrete and unique *you*? Or is it, rather, that person who maintains the *I do* once given to a concrete man/woman, marches forward with him or her, and in this *I do* never succumbs to stagnation but, with always greater profundity, learns to freely surrender to the *you* and, in this process, liberates him- or herself?

In this context the problem of the modern attitude toward the child also arises, because marriage becomes family through the children. Given that, according to the Christian conception, marital love between woman and man cannot be secluded or revolve around itself, but surpasses itself by means of the children and for their cause, the love between man and woman and the transmission of life form an indissoluble whole. With the children, the parents are entrusted with responsibility for the future, so that to a great extent the future of humanity depends on the family: "Without the family there is no future, but aging of the society, an evident danger for occidental societies."[3] This process is taking place today because couples, above all in Europe, hardly want children anymore. The most extreme reason people find having children unacceptable is that, for some, the future has become so insecure that they ask themselves in anguish, "How can one bring a new life into an unknown future?" In more than a biological sense, people can only transmit human life responsibly when they can also pass on life in an integral sense—more precisely, when they can transmit a meaning that holds up even in life's crises and a hope that is stronger than all the unknowns of the future. Because of this, people will transmit life and will confide in an uncertain future only if they again delve deeply into the mystery of life and, in this process, recognize that the only sure capital in facing the future is the human being himself.

From this perspective it is comprehensible that the problem of the family is, in reality, the problem of the human being himself and that the present questioning of the familial institution represents also an attack on the Christian idea of the human being, as already diagnosed in the 1980s by then-cardinal Joseph Ratzinger: "The struggle for the human being is undergone today in large measure as the struggle for or against the family."[4] In the attitude regarding the family comes to light, not least, the way in which the human being understands himself. The decision in favor of the family contains an unequivocal message: conjugal fidelity between two people and the consequent surrender in love and the transmission of life do not represent any threat or loss of human freedom but its authentic realization. If the highest possibility of human freedom consists in making definitive decisions, only that person who is capable of true faithfulness is capable of becoming authentically free, and only he who is himself free can be truly faithful. Faithfulness is the price that must be paid for freedom, and freedom is the price that faithfulness earns. The Christian can see realized this style of life by the Holy Family as its prototypical model of free faithfulness and faithful freedom, and for this style of life it is a "marvelous example."

THE REALITY OF CREATION
AND MYSTERY OF SALVATION

With the reference to the Holy Family, it is in no way intended to affirm that marriage and family are exclusively Christian realities and, consequently, only realizable in the faith. They are, rather, originating institutions of humanity and belong first and foremost to the order of the creation. Jesus himself demonstrates this with unequivocal clarity when, in disputing with the Pharisees about the possibility of divorce and about the authorization foreseen by Moses to extend the act of repudiation, he harks back to times before the historical establishment of the law in Israel and refers to the creation itself: "But from the beginning it was not so. And I say to you, whoever divorces his wife, except for unchastity, and marries another commits adultery" (Matt 19:8–9). With his recourse to "the beginning," Jesus expresses unequivocally that marriage and family have their foundation already in the creation willed by God.

The conjugal relationship between woman and man, according to the priestly narrative of the creation, is so fundamental that it is even incorporated into a theological definition of human essence: "So God created humankind in his image, in the image of God he created them; male and female he created them" (Gen 1:27). In this radical sense, *the* human being doesn't exist; the human being exists, rather, only as male and female, and sexual differentiation forms part of the definition of human according to the order of the creation.

Only in the mutual reference of the one to the other and in the bond of the one with the other do human beings find the definition of their meaning and are image of God. That the human being precisely has not been created as a singular being is driven home by the Yahwist narration of the creation with the expression, full of mercy, of Yahweh to Adam: "It is not good that the man should be alone; I will make him a helper as his partner" (Gen 2:18).

This basic natural reality of marriage and family is the foundation for, in the Holy Scripture, the relation between woman and man coming to serve, in turn, as symbol of the alliance of God with humanity and as model of his love and fidelity. The matrimonial union between man and woman is the visible representation of that wedding that God celebrates with his humanity and with all of his creation. It is, so to speak, like the "grammar" of the order of the creation, with whose help can be expressed in words, in a way intelligible to the human being, the love and the fidelity of God. That's why, already in the Old Testament, conjugal fidelity serves as image of God's fidelity in his alliance and, on the contrary, adultery is seen as sign and result of the human being's infidelity to God.

What is already contained in the meaning of marriage and family, such as is derived from the order of the creation, has its ultimate significance only with the insertion of the order of creation into the order of salvation through the event of Christ—the order in which matrimony is subsumed in the new being "in Christ," which has its foundation in baptism and, therefore, is realized "in the Lord" (1 Cor 7:39).[5] In the Letter to the Ephesians, principally, the natural Old Testament order of matrimony is referred to the mystery of the relation of Christ with his Church. First, it recalls the Old Testament affirmation—"For this reason a man will leave his father and mother and be joined to his wife, and the two will become one flesh"—and later it is understood as a christological prophecy and reread in the light of the Christian faith: "This is a great mystery, and I am applying it to Christ and the church" (Eph 5:31–32). In this mystery, the Letter to the Ephesians uncovers the hidden meaning of the citation taken from the Old Testament Book of Genesis, and perceives matrimony itself as a "mystery." Given that the word *mystery*—in Greek, *mysterion*—signifies, in biblical tradition, the eternal salvational will of God, which historically has become reality in a definitive manner in Jesus Christ, it is expressed thereby that the mutual surrender of woman and man is not only the image of the surrender of the life of Jesus Christ to his Church but, also, and above all, the sacramental sign that makes present the love and the fidelity of God, which has been gratuitously given to us in Jesus Christ in an unequaled way.

That which from "the beginning" of the world has been a reality of the good creation made by God, namely, the matrimonial alliance of woman and man, in the New Testament is converted into sacrament of the alliance of God with mankind that has reached its perfection in Jesus Christ and, by this, is converted into a sign that makes present the mystery of Christ and the Church. According to this, the New Testament vision of marriage and family contains a new message "which makes the commitment of the beginning a possibility of the present in the faith and inserts it in the context of the faith, such that matrimony can rise to the order of the faith, or in other words: acquires its order and meaning insofar as lived in faith and starting from this faith."[6]

NATURAL FAMILY AND
GREAT FAMILY OF GOD

With this the intimate relation maintained between marriage/family and Church has been made clear. From the christological vision of marriage and family in the Letter to the Ephesians, it is just a small step, on the one hand, to understand the life of the Church as cut from the same pattern of familial life and the Church herself as family,[7] and, on the other, to perceive the family as the basic cell of the Church and as "domestic Church."[8] As the individual Christian belongs by birth to a natural family and by baptism to the great family of God, and as, consequently, birth and new birth in baptism form a unity, likewise for the Christian faith also, the natural family and the great family of God form a whole. On one side, the singular Christian family—called by God to be community of love—is the smallest basic cell of the Church, which in the language of the tradition is qualified as a "domestic Church." But on the other side, the singular Christian family can only subsist, in the last analysis, with the support of the great family of the Church, which offers it a protecting shelter.

Bethlehem and Nazareth as Models

That the Christian family as domestic Church, and the Church as new family of God are very closely related is already clear in the Holy Family. Ancient Christian iconography, in any case, saw the Holy Family in the stable at Christmas as prototype of the Christian family and as primordial figure of the Church. The Church is represented, above all, in the figure of Mary, who is the image and reflection of the Church and gives the Church her true measure: the Church and the Christian family have to adjust to her time and again, because Mary herself adjusted fully to the measure of Jesus Christ. Facing her is St. Joseph, whom tradition has presented as high priest and, consequently, as model of the Christian bishop. The blossoming staff that in many representations St. Joseph holds has been interpreted in this sense: like Joseph, the bishop is also constituted as administrator of the mystery of God, as father of family and guardian of the sanctuary that is the stable. As Mary and the child are under the protection of Joseph, likewise the Church is entrusted and given to the bishop as spouse. The Church, therefore, is not at all at the disposition or even at the mercy of the bishop's power, but under his protective custody.

The stable of the nativity is not a simple folkloric representation of the faith: it leads to the most intimate center of the mystery of Christmas, in which the Holy Family also represents the mystery of the Church. This applies especially to the life of the Holy Family in Nazareth, in which we have been given the model of Christian familial life. Because in Nazareth, that is to say, in the Galilee of the Gentiles, Jesus grew up as a believing Jew: without schooling, he learned the Holy Scripture in the house in which the Word of God found its home. Given that we Christians live today in the modern "Galilee of the Gentiles," we're on the right track if we discover and consider the family as Church, which matters a lot, also and precisely today, to the life of faith in the families. It must be continually kept in mind that the New Testament did not commence in the temple, or even on the Holy Mount, but in the small house of the Virgin in Nazareth. As the life of Jesus, in the beginning, developed in the house of Mary and in the home of the workman Joseph, likewise the Church, in the modern "Galilee of the Gentiles," has to retake, once and again, Nazareth as her point of departure; the Church "cannot grow or give fruit if she does not come to understand that her secret roots are safe in the atmosphere of Nazareth."[9] In the Holy Family, in Nazareth, the Church can and must find still today her ideal model and assume her priestly responsibility for the life of the faith.

The Holy Family as a Community in the Will of God

The reflections that we have developed up to here could easily give rise to the impression that Nazareth would be the peaceful idyll of a family life without problems. But this impression is corrected with the fact that those responsible for the liturgical calendar have chosen as Gospel for the Feast of the Holy Family the passage of the boy Jesus in the temple at the age of twelve (Luke 2:41–52), in which a serious conflict appears between Jesus and his parents. On the one hand, the profound uneasiness of Mary, for her Son, is summarized in the word—*why*—that says it all: "Child, why have you treated us like this? Look, your father and I have been searching for you in great anxiety." On the other hand, Jesus shows no sign of comprehension or regret; he responds unexpectedly with a counterquestion with which, in turn, he blames his parents for their incomprehension: "Why were you searching for me? Did you not know that I must be in my Father's house?" What produces in us the impression of a serious conflict between the will of the parents and the will of Jesus is, upon closer examination, a common effort to know what, in the last analysis, is God's will for Jesus and for his parents. Only thus can be perceived the true nature and, in a certain way, the dramatic fundamental situation of the Holy Family that, at bottom, is a community seeking the will of God, and so listens to the word of God and lives with it.

This happens in a special way in Mary, the mother of Jesus, who in the Holy Scripture is presented as model of life with the Word of God. In Mary we encounter that woman of stalwart faith who fully receives in herself the word of God to give it to the world, and who, even after the birth of the Word of God, pondered in her heart every word that came from God. The Evangelist Luke especially describes Mary as a person who was all ears for the word of God. Already in the annunciation of the birth of Jesus it is said that Mary was troubled by the greeting of the angel and "pondered what sort of greeting this might be" (Luke 1:29). In Greek, the Evangelist's word here translated as "pondered" points to the word *dialogue*. With this it is meant that Mary entered into personal and intimate conversation with the Word of God, who comes to her aid, enters into silent dialogue with her, and tries to unravel its deep meaning. Mary behaves in an analogous way in the nativity story, following the adoration of the child by the shepherds in the stable: "Mary treasured all these words and pondered them in her heart" (Luke 2:19). Mary translates the event of the nativity in Bethlehem into word, and she immerses herself in this word so that it may, in her heart, be converted into seed. Luke recalls this image a third time in the scene of the twelve-year-old Jesus in the temple: "His mother treasured all these things in her heart" (Luke 2:51). In truth, only the following phrase gives to this affirmation all of its explosive force: "They did not understand what he said to them." By this, Luke wants to make clear that even for believers and, therefore, people open to God, the word of God is not always immediately intelligible. Patience and humility, then, are necessary: the humility with which Mary receives within her heart that which she at first didn't understand and lets it act in the most profound intimacy in order to be able to process it.

With these three scenes, the Evangelist shows us that Mary was all ears for the Word of God and was so receptive that this Word could become flesh in her, as St. Augustine observed: "Before becoming mother according to the flesh, she was already mother according to the spirit."

In this fundamental attitude of seeking the will of God in his word, Mary is model and prototype of the Church, or, more precisely, "Church at root."[10] As model of the Church, Mary shows in an exemplary way the relationship that the Church has to cultivate with the word of God; she also shows that the Church, in the very first place, is a Marian Church and, only starting from there and in her service, a Petrine Church, as expressed graphically by the Catholic theologian Urs von Balthasar: "In Mary, the Church already exists corporally, in person, before being organized in Peter."[11] The personalization of the Church in Mary consists here in the consequent ordering of her life according to God's will.

This same fundamental attitude of Mary characterized St. Joseph. He also had felt the challenge, in a life situation by no means easy, to explore the will of God, because, in the society of that time, to be in love with a pregnant woman was a public scandal. To normalize this surprising relationship with Mary, two paths were open to him in accordance with the law of the time: he could have either solicited before the tribunal the punishment of Mary according to law, which is to say, stoning; or he could have turned Mary away forever with a letter of repudiation. But both solutions would have resulted in Mary's disgrace and the impediment of God's salvational plan. In face of this dilemma, Joseph at first thought of separating in all secret from Mary, because he didn't want to compromise her—the reason for which the Evangelist Matthew expressly qualifies Joseph as "just." However, at the same time, Joseph was open to a much greater project, about which, in any case, he could find out only through an angel who told him in dreams, "Joseph, son of David, do not be afraid to take Mary as your wife, for the child conceived in her is from the Holy Spirit." (Matt 1:20). Because Joseph perceived in this voice the will of God, and responded to it in obedience, he became the authentic "witness of the nativity." For in him, "the message of the Nativity arrives at its goal, to wit: to the objective response, the believing affirmation of the *agape* of God and to the obedient life starting from this *agape*."[12] The nativity was made possible because Joseph listened to the voice of the angel and, following God's indication, which he heard in this voice, obeyed; and he did so silently and discreetly, for which Alfred Delp has rightly qualified him as "the man of silent help."

The Family of Jesus under the Cross

If we let the figures of Mary and Joseph work on us in this light, the Holy Family presents itself to us as "marvelous example" because it let itself be guided totally by the will of God. The Holy Family had to demonstrate this attitude over and over and, above all, precisely in face of the behavior of their own Son, who so raised the decisive criterion of life according to God's will that he could relativize even biological descent and familial relations and, by this, the family itself.

Thus, for example, to his family's desire to see him, Jesus responded with the programmatic declaration, "My mother and my brothers are those who hear the word of God and do it" (Luke 8:21).

At first, this word of Jesus produces a somewhat acrid impression, the same as does the response that, in the wedding of Cana, he gives to Mary, who had realized that the hosts had run out of wine, felt their anxiousness, and directed herself confidently to Jesus. From him, however, she received an anything but gentle response: "Woman, what concern is that to you and to me? My hour has not yet come" (John 2:4). In this scene, it can especially cause irritation that Jesus would treat his own mother simply as "woman." The deeper significance of this manner of directing himself to her can be discovered only by starting from another fact: in the Gospel of John, Jesus again treats his mother as "woman" precisely at the foot of the cross, when, referring to John, he says to Mary, "Woman, here is your son" (John 19:26). By this, the Evangelist John indicates that only on the cross has the "hour" arrived—that which in the wedding at Cana Jesus said had not yet arrived, has arrived as the hour of the definitive wedding of God and humanity. On the cross, the human wedding at Cana is elevated to symbol of that moment in which the wedding between God and man takes place—more exactly, to the "symbol of the divine wedding festival, to which the Father invites by means of the Son and in which the gift of the plenitude of the good is given, symbolized by the abundance of wine."[13]

Only by this profound symbolism of the wedding is discovered the significance of Jesus' treatment of his mother by calling her "woman." By it, the Gospel of John expresses not only the singular and unique position of Mary in the history of salvation but indicates, furthermore, that Jesus gives priority to the spiritual bond over human relationship. Only from this perspective is also clarified what Jesus accomplished, at the foot of the cross, between Mary and John (John 19:25–27). Jesus, seeing his mother at the beloved disciple's side, says to his mother: "Woman, here is your son." Then he says to the disciple, "Here is your mother." This signifies, on the one hand, that Jesus, in the hour of the cross, has consummated his mission: upon returning to the Father in heaven, he leaves him behind, with the giving of his mother to the son—"Here is your mother"—the "first fruit of the new family" that was to constitute the "embryo of the Church and of the new humanity."[14] As between those who are in love the mother of one becomes also the mother of the other, likewise Jesus entrusts to his disciple and, with him, to all of the disciples who in this way become children of his mother, the most valuable that he could entrust: his own mother. In the hour of the cross, on the other hand, the maternity of Mary, which had begun with the "fiat" in Nazareth, also reached its zenith, inasmuch as, with Jesus' giving her the disciple—"Here is your son"—her maternity extends to all men and women; in this way, Mary becomes Mother of the Church. When, in conclusion, the Gospel of John says that "from that hour" the disciple took her to his house, this event can be seen as the most profound root of the Church as new family of Jesus. The Church sprang forth exactly in the moment that Jesus entrusted John to Mary's care and gave Mary to John. In the new bond of union between Mary—the mother—and John—the disciple—that Jesus established from upon the cross, thus indissolubly linking at the same time the divine maternity of Mary with her maternity regarding the Church, is the originating nucleus of the new family of Jesus Christ, which without doubt was the objective of his terrestrial mission.

Jesus Gathers the New Family

That the terrestrial mission of Jesus consisted in gathering together the eschatological people of God and, with this, the new family of God, is expressed above all in the formation of the circle of the twelve. Immediately, at the beginning of his public activity, Jesus gathered disciples around him and from them chose twelve witnesses, whose call the Evangelist Mark describes with the energetic expression that Jesus "appointed" the twelve (Mark 3:14). With the institution of the twelve, Jesus revealed his mission in Israel—which was understood as the people of the twelve tribes—and that, in anticipation of the messianic salvational time, he expected above all the restoration of the twelve tribes of Israel, those that had arisen from the twelve sons of Jacob. Jesus, on "appointing" the twelve, gave it to be understood that he understood himself as the new Jacob who, with the twelve, laid the foundations of the new Israel. With this, Jesus presented himself as the patriarch of the new people of God, whose foundation and origin the twelve instituted. Thus, Jesus signaled the beginning of a new family in the new alliance in such a manner that it is necessary to share the judgment of Gerhard Lohfink, Catholic exegete of the New Testament: "The person of Jesus and the figure of the Twelve is the new in the New Testament."[15] The importance that the twelve had in the intention of Jesus can be deduced from the fact that in the first Church, after the betrayal of Judas, their number is completed with the posterior election of Matthias (Acts 1:15–26).

The determination of the meaning of the twelve becomes even easier if one asks what it was that Jesus intended and wanted with their institution. The Evangelist Mark describes this by saying that Jesus made the twelve "to be with him, and to be sent out to proclaim the message, and to have authority to cast out demons" (Mark 3:14–15). This description signifies that the new family of Jesus is born from the "be-with-him" that the disciples have received from him and for whose transmission to other people he has sent them. In this event of the call can already be seen a precise description of what the Church can and must be as new family of God: "There is Church, on the one hand, in order to 'be-with-him' and to the extent that she is by and with him; also, on the other hand, to take part in his mission and to be available to be sent by the Lord."[16]

With this it is clear that the new family of Jesus is no longer formed through biological descent but with the personal call made by Jesus. In the first Church, this occurred in baptism, in which a person surrendered existentially to Jesus as his new Lord. Upon the neophyte's entering into the existence of the Son, proper to Jesus, he enters at the same time into the great family of those who together with him are its children. Since the to be-in-Christ, through the gift of baptism, is identical to the to be-in-the-body-of-Christ, the adoption of the person as child of God that happens in baptism is at the same time reception in the great family of God and, with this, incorporation, as brothers and sisters, in his body. With emphasis, Paul insists on this indissoluble connection between baptism and Church: "For in the one Spirit we were all baptized into one body—Jews or Greeks, slaves or free—and we were all made to drink of one Spirit" (1 Cor 12:13).

That in the new family of Jesus biological descent is no longer decisive is demonstrated above all in the Last Supper, which must be interpreted as seal of the alliance and, consequently, as the concrete founding of his new family, which is only truly constituted as new family in relation to the alliance with God. In the eucharistic deed, human bloodlines no longer count; the new family is constituted, rather, through the communion of blood that the disciples have with Jesus. This eucharistic perspective is deepened through the ulterior recognition that Jesus celebrated his Passover with his disciples. As the Passover of Israel was a family festival and therefore was not celebrated in the temple but in the family home, likewise Jesus celebrated the Passover with the disciples who were constituted in his new family. In fidelity to the intention of Jesus and to his Passover, in the primitive Church the Eucharist constituted the central Christian festival of the family.

Church as a Family and Family as the Domestic Church

With these few indications it should be clear that the Church and the family maintain a relation so intimate that the Church understands herself as family and the family is the embryo of the Church and, in this sense, is domestic Church. This mutual relationship is recalled by a custom that is backed by a long tradition. We are accustomed to each church having the name of a saint and being consecrated to this name. Behind this custom of assigning a name to ecclesiastical buildings and treating them, in a sense, as persons is hidden in reality a profound significance, because in the most ancient times of Christianity, it was not the churches that were designated with a name but the family homes in which Christians met to read the Holy Scripture and celebrate the Eucharist. Until the third century, Christians did not dispose of any space proper to the cult, but met in private houses that bore the name of their owner. Thus, for example, Paul informs us of a certain Gaius in Corinth "who is host to me and to the whole church" (Rom 16:23), and of a Nympha of Laodicea and of "the church in her house" (Col 4:15). When in later times these houses were converted into church buildings, the names of those who had put their homes at the disposition of Christian meetings were maintained, and since then they became the patrons of the respective communities and their ecclesiastic buildings.

This old custom reminds us, even today, that in the community of Christian faith, the Church of stone is not decisive but rather the Church is composed of people who, like stones, assemble to form the living building of the Church. These stones have to adjust to one another in such a way that from them a solid construction arises. This is only possible when such people, as St. Augustine emphasized, are configured by love, and by love, united among themselves.[17] Mutual love constitutes the material with which the building of God is raised up. In this sense, the custom alluded to recalls that the first Christians met in family homes and, at the same time, that the Church in the original sense was domestic Church and that the family constitutes the embryo of the Church. To the great commitment of Christian spouses and families is owed above all that, in the beginning, the Christian faith could extend so rapidly, as Pope Benedict XVI has so beautifully explained: Christianity "could grow thanks not only to the apostles who announced it. To take root in the terrain of the people, to develop vitally, the commitment of those families was necessary, of those spouses, of those Christian communities, of the Christian laity: they offered the 'fertilized soil' for the growth of the faith. And the Church grows always only in this way."[18]

THE CHRISTIAN FAMILY AS
THE SCHOOL OF LIFE AND FAITH

In this sense, to conclude, it must be asked what mission corresponds to the Christian family, as the smallest form of the Church, and in line with this, as domestic Church, if it is contemplated in light of the mystery of faith of the Holy Family, presented to the natural family as well as to the new family of God as a "marvelous example." The clearest way to delimit this mission consists in characterizing the Christian family as an elemental school of life and faith, in the sense that has been detailed by the teaching of the Church:[19] "All family members exercise, in keeping with the role proper to each one, the priesthood received in baptism and cooperate so that the family constitutes a community of grace and prayer, a school of human and Christian virtue, and a space for the first announcement of the faith to the children" (*Catechism of the Catholic Church* 350).

As the Holy Family sought God's will in everything, and considered everything in the light of faith, so is the family today called first of all to be a school of faith and thereby domestic Church in the proper sense. As children, in daily life, learn the mother tongue as the first and most important language, they likewise first learn the language of faith in their parent's house. To be able to act as school of faith, the Christian family would do well to learn something from the Jewish religion, because this is a religion that is lived primarily and basically in the families and owes to this circumstance its robust capacity of resistance, especially in the great vicissitudes of its history. In Christianity as well, the religious socialization in the family figures as something of primary necessity, especially in the modern European societies that are increasingly forgetting and losing the memory of their cultural "mother tongue"—that is to say, the culture molded by Christianity. Thence the Christian family constitutes a privileged space in which the faith can and must be experienced and transmitted to the coming generation, because what is neglected in this primary ambience cannot be made up for by other institutions like the school or the catechism that, finally, have only a secondary character. The charge of the transmission of the faith will consist above all in that the children learn the basic language of the Christian faith, that is, the language of prayer; the best way to achieve this will be that the children perceive their parents as people of prayer and, thus, as witnesses of the incommensurate love that God professes to each person.

As in the center of the Holy Family is found the child whom Mary and Joseph protect and care for as sanctuary, so also is the Christian family called to be school and sanctuary of life, and this in a double sense. A Christian family is characterized, in the first place, by an opening, both in principle and in fact, to the child. Because Christians are convinced that especially in the transmission of life is reflected the love of God for the human being, the Christian family is the fundamental space in which the person learns to receive and give love gratuitously. Hence Christian parents consider their children the most precious good of the family; with this they set a prophetic countersign against the rapid and progressive regression of the birthrate in European societies that cannot but be qualified as "demographic winter," and the dramatic demonstration of the want of confidence in life and the lack of hope for the future. In the second place, the Christian family can be perceived also as "sanctuary of life" because in it is alive and irradiating toward society the conviction of the sacred and, hence, the inviolable character of human life from conception to natural death.

When the Christian family is at the service of the transmission of the faith and the transmission of human life, it is then shown also to be a school of humanism in which the child can grow up to become truly a person; then it is also at the service of the humanization of human society, whose fundamental cell is to be considered the family. The Church, upon committing to the dignity of the family as the most elemental structure of human society that proceeds from the love between a woman and a man and that is open to the transmission of life, makes also an indispensable contribution to a promising future for humanity. For marriage and family are not outworn ideas or outdated institutions; on the contrary, today the future of humanity also depends on the family.

To testify to this liberating vision in the societies of today constitutes the urgent mission of the Church as family and of the family as domestic Church. This testimony will be all the more believable the more that Christian churches give it in ecumenical communion, as has now been possible to do, in an exemplary manner, with the Orthodox Churches;[20] for the Christian family can irradiate within modern society only if the gospel of the family is witnessed in ecumenical cooperation. For this, the orientation of the Holy Family, as "marvelous example," is invitation and aid.

8

FIVE REMINDERS FROM THE PERSPECTIVE OF THE SHEPHERD OF SOULS

On the Pastoral Program for the Divorced and Civilly Remarried Faithful

CHRISTOPH SCHÖNBORN

❦

As Christians we are encouraged to be close to the poorest of the poor. The Second Vatican Council demands that attention be given to the poorest, above all in the curate of souls in the parishes. The poorest are not only those who lack means of life or are excluded, but also those who have failed in love, who have had problems in an initiated love relationship, or have seen the home that they constructed crumble. In our parishes there are many divorced faithful who have remarried civilly:[1] they participate in different groups, collaborate actively in the preparation of the sacraments, are involved in charitable activities, attend the Eucharist, and would like to take communion. For many of these people it is also a necessity to also give an example to their children. This poses a difficult problem for many shepherds of souls: How can we help

171

mercifully those whose heart, frequently, is torn and who wish to construct a life with more love than the previous one had?

In the funeral rites of Austrian federal president Thomas Klestil, I spoke of the dilemma that many people today are facing and that Thomas Klestil also faced: "It does not correspond to us to judge. Jesus said it emphatically: 'Do not judge, so that you may not be judged' (Matt 7:1). Let us never forget these words of Jesus. With consternation we observe how great the longing is today to experience a fulfilling relationship, the longing for security in marriage and the family, and how difficult it has become to see these longings satisfied. You always respected the position of the Church on this question, though it wasn't easy for you. Neither is it easy for the Church to find the way between the necessary protection of marriage and family, on one hand, and the equally necessary mercy toward human failure and the attempts to begin anew, on the other. Perhaps your death, dear friend, may provide us with the occasion to work all together for one another, aware that both of these are necessary and that neither of them is simple."[2]

In Austria many know that I myself come from a broken family. My parents divorced when I was thirteen. They met during the war and after just three days were married; my father was at the front and felt the perfectly understandable need to know that there was someone at home while he was in Stalingrad. The war ended and it very soon became clear that this house was not built on a solid foundation; nevertheless, my parents stayed together until 1958.

I speak, then, of a reality that I know from personal experience, a reality that likewise comes out to meet me from many flanks, for at least in our European countries and in

North America it is a daily question. But also it is necessary to broaden the view and observe those people who don't marry, but simply live together. If we look at other continents, we see an even more dramatic situation. In Latin America, not a few men have various wives and children with whom they live in irregular circumstances. In Africa, polygamy continues to be very extensive in numerous places. All over the place we have to deal with problems related to this fundamental human reality. From the first page in the Bible, the union of man and woman to form a family and transmit life is highly valued. At the same time, the Bible treats of the conflicts that from the "fall," that is, from the original sin, have weighed upon the relations between man and woman.

I invite above all to take a merciful view. We all know complex biographies, patchwork families. Not long ago I had a long and serious conversation with a man who was married for the fourth time and had children from his first three relationships. The fourth marriage is, at last, a happy relationship; the couple has been living together for seventeen years now, and he discovered the faith only a few years ago. He is content to have found faith for his life, but is burdened with the failure of his three previous marriages. What must be done with this person who has ended up finding Christ and discovering the faith and is now fully integrated in the parish community? He only wants to know one thing: "Now that I'm a believer, can I participate fully in the life of the Church and receive the sacraments?" In his former life this played no role whatsoever.

The first thing that we cannot overlook is that believing and united families are the exception is our society. They are not the normal case. In the city of Vienna, divorces are normal, and often second or third marriages. As a result of this, complex familial situations arise, the so-called patchwork families. But there are people who don't remarry. In France, thanks to the PACS (Civil Pact of Solidarity), there is a *light* marriage, a registered de facto union (as there is in Spain). In France it is not so much the homosexual couples who make use of this legal recourse, but rather the heterosexual couples who opt for a less weighty form of relationship, because they're afraid of the burden of marriage and the obligations that it brings, somewhat like the possibility of a business failure.

These patchwork families present without doubt abundant problems to all involved. But we cannot overlook that often there is also much good in these situations.[3] The basic condition for priests and shepherds of souls is not to treat these marriages or couples with a condemning attitude, but with empathy, even when they find themselves already in their third, fourth, or fifth stable couple relationship and have children here and there or even abortions behind them. Let us not forget: in the families composed of patches there is often much generosity; this is not the exclusive property of our good families who remain united for life. In these existential situations it is necessary to see the bruised reed that has not yet broken and the smoldering wick still unquenched (cf. Isa 42:3; Matt 12:20), although from an objective point of view the circumstances are irregular. If we don't modify our view regarding these situations, we will be converted into a sect! We Christians are a minority, and marriages that live together in mutual fidelity represent a small group in the large urban agglomerations, but now very often also in rural zones where people lead a Christian life and even understand the sacrament of matrimony. In Vienna, about 50 percent of the marriages end in divorce and many of those affected later remarry (more or less 35 percent of weddings celebrated).[4] This data doesn't even take into account the elevated number of couples who simply live together without ever marrying. The number of weddings celebrated by the Church has descended dramatically.

How must we proceed pastorally in this situation? I have formulated a program of five points for priests and shepherds of souls in the diocese of Vienna: *Die spirituelle, christliche und mensliche Begleitung von geschiedenen und wiederver-heiratenten Paaren* (The spiritual, Christian, and human accompaniment of divorced and remarried couples).[5] It's a type of aid for reading the reality, of steps that help to travel a road of accompaniment with those affected, and can lead to a true conversion, to an authentic renewal of the life of faith. In this program the following groups of problems are contemplated.

WHO IS MERCIFUL WITH THE CHILDREN?

In the vision of Jesus, in the gospel, the poorest, the little ones, and the helpless always count the most. Who are the poor in the vital circumstances of these patchwork families? It is not those who have remarried, for they have found a new companion; from a human viewpoint, sidestepping the rules of the Church, they now find themselves in a situation in which they have become "entangled." The first victims of our divorces are the children. To those who criticize, "Ah, the Church is too hard on the divorced who have remarried," it is necessary to respond, "No! The Church is compassionate with the children." Where is there a lobby, a pressure group for the children of divorced parents? Where is the voice of public opinion that says, "The first victims are the children of broken couples"? They have a daddy and a mommy, and then suddenly is added an "uncle," an "aunt," daddy's friend, mommy's friend. And how often do the divorced lay on their children the burden of their conjugal conflict? Who notices more often the domestic *War of Roses* (for the famous movie directed in 1989 by Danny DeVito)?

Frequently there are grave sins in this sense, and it becomes necessary to remind, "Don't burden your children with your personal problems! They must not be hostages of your discords. To convert them into hostages is a crime against the souls of the little ones." When I say this before the congregated community, there always follows a profound silence: Where is there mercy toward the children? So then, my first question to the divorced who have remarried is, "What is the situation of your children? Have you made them suffer because of your conflicts? What harm have you inflicted on them? Have you repented for it and have you asked forgiveness, both from God and from your children, for the injustice that you have done them?" Most children dream—consciously or unconsciously—of putting their parents' home back together (I know whereof I speak), although with the intellect they know that this will never happen.

THOSE WHO END UP ALONE, FORGOTTEN BY THE GENERAL RULE

Which of the two divorced spouses is counted among those who end up alone, among those who don't find a new companion? After divorcing, one does not automatically find a new companion; the man has perhaps more probabilities to find a new mate, but the woman usually has custody of the children. How many women, but also men, remain alone because their spouse has abandoned them? Surely at some time in your life you have spoken with "homeless" people, men and women who live in the street; they are usually men. When they are asked how they have come to this situation, an identical pattern almost always appears: they divorced; they were obliged to leave the family home; they have nowhere to live; they have to pay the children's pension, but they can't manage to; they are disoriented because they lack a home; they start to drink, if they didn't already; and this leads them to the abyss.

How many women are condemned to solitude because their husbands left them for someone younger? Our society overflows with the solitude of wives who have been left in the lurch or are victims of divorce. Who speaks of these women? The gospel always takes the side of the weakest, of the little ones; consequently, we must become spokesmen, a lobby or pressure group, defenders of these solitary women who end up alone and don't find a new mate. Is the Church unmerciful with the divorced who have remarried civilly? Divorce is very often a terrible work of destruction, including the economic effect. There are highly interesting studies on the dramatic economic consequences of divorce. How many small family businesses have gone belly up in the moment that the family that sustained them failed?

No. The Church is not unmerciful, since it pays attention to the children and to the spouses who are victims of divorce. Has there been at least an attempt of reconciliation with the spouse who ended up alone? What meaning can access to the sacraments have if all this pain remains without reconciliation, if at least some effort to reconcile is not made?

HAS THE HISTORY OF BLAME BEEN FACED?

Blame always exists in cases of divorce. Have the spouses tried at least to mutually forgive, to reach pardon, if only in part, to put an end to the war of divorce? How can a new relationship be built, a new bond, upon hate—often full of bitterness—the remains of the first marriage? The shepherds of souls who accompany the divorced must undertake this attempt with them. "Have you at least taken some step toward your former spouse, your exwife, your exhusband, after the divorce? What does the desire for the sacraments signify if the old hate and the old conflict are still alive?"

THE FAITHFUL SPOUSES: IGNORED?

In the parishes and communities there are families that remain heroically united in spite of all the storms and squalls, because they have promised fidelity and because they take the sacrament seriously. What sign are the priests and shepherds of souls giving them if they speak all the time about the "poor divorced and remarried"? Certainly it is necessary to show compassion for these, but beware: let this not lead us to forget to express encouragement, recognition, and gratitude to those marriages that last, for they last in the faith. A deacon, whom the bishop entrusts to accompany those in the diocese who have divorced and remarried, as well as marriages that are going through difficulties or who are about to divorce, testifies that the Lord, by way of accompaniment, can save marriages and couples. If in our ecclesial communities we were to point out the couples who live their marriage in mutual faithfulness and offer an example of the significance of God's faithfulness toward us, this would encourage the younger marriages not to part ways at the first sign of trouble, and the not so young to endure. How often we see divorces after twenty-five or even forty years of conjugal life! How moving it is, on the other hand, to participate in the celebration of a golden or diamond wedding anniversary!

How can we present as models those who remain faithful to their wedding vows? And how must we respond to the divorced when they complain of the Church's callousness? It is necessary to ask ourselves if the shepherd of souls might not walk at their side, accompany them, and say to them, "Look at this or that couple in our community, in our parish: how they remain united despite the difficulties! Unfortunately you have not been able to stay together with your wives or husbands; your marriage has failed, but don't accuse the Church of lack of compassion. Look first at yourselves and then supplicate Jesus mercy for you and for all those who suffer because of your divorce and your new marriage."

CONSCIENCE BEFORE GOD

I always say to the divorced and remarried, "Even if you achieve the annulment of your first marriage and even if your priest administers—though hesitatingly—the sacraments to you, because your second marriage is a reality and because you have the profound and sincere desire to unite with Christ through the sacraments, the question will invariably remain, How will you present yourself before God, before your conscience, in the depths of your heart? God cannot be deceived—false appearances are worthless before him."

In our conscience we are alone before God. Before him we must pose this question: Have I been merciful to my spouse; and to our children? These questions cannot be excused by any priest, by any Church. They can only be answered before God.

It's very difficult to decide how to approach such situations. I'm aware of this.

We must exclude two extremes. The first: a parish priest in a neighboring diocese hung a large poster in his Church: "Here, everyone can take communion." This is not a pastoral attitude nor is it the attitude of a good shepherd of souls. It's false mercy. We all need to travel the road of conversion. The other extreme consists in saying, "There's no solution for the divorced, or for those who remarry, under no circumstances, never." Neither is a satisfactory path.

It is necessary to consider each situation close up, in the context of the cure of souls. I know that this is very difficult. Many priests, shepherds of souls, and those affected need clear rules. It is, without doubt, the rule of Jesus, the gospel, and this is very clear. On one occasion, while visiting a parish, a man addressed me in a rather aggressive tone of voice: "Why is the Church so callous? It lacks all compassion with the divorced and remarried." "Dear friend," I responded, "how the Church would like to have a solution to this problem. But Jesus Christ made his opinion known in this respect. That's the obstacle!" And then, I simply cited the words of Jesus: "Anyone who divorces his wife and marries another commits adultery" (Luke 16:18; Mark 10:11; Matt 19:9). The man turned pale and didn't say anything; these words had gone directly to his heart: "You are this man, Jesus tells him, and you have broken the promise of faithfulness that you made." When this moment arrives, then merciful forgiveness can occur. This is effective only in the truth; in the lie it has no effect. While one remains anchored in the accusation of others, Jesus cannot offer his mercy.

First it must be seen whether some path of faith exists. In my book on the Eucharist I mention the example of a couple in which the woman is divorced and remarried.[7] Both the husband and his wife accept that they can neither confess nor take communion, and they do this from fidelity to the doctrine and the word of Jesus. This peasant family has eight children, whom they have educated admirably in the faith. I know them well. The parents never approach to receive the sacraments, but when the children take communion they say, "Mom, today I take this for you." When I asked this lady, "Don't you long to receive the communion?" her answer was, "Of course I do, and very much; but when the people of our parish community tell me that the Church has become more liberal and that now I could take communion, I answer them, 'Don't worry about me; worry instead about those who could receive the sacraments but don't.'" Here are examples of impressive behaviors, and it is important to encourage such people on this, their way, which amounts to a blessing for the Church.

But there are also those for whom such an attitude seems unreachable. They often suffer bitterly because they know themselves excluded from the sacraments. Their questions then become more tormented, and their requests more insistent. Is there no path of reconciliation for people whose marriage has failed? It is proposed that we adopt the "solution" of the Orthodox Churches, who accept up to three unions with divorce and new marriage (though only the first wedding is considered full ecclesial sacrament). The Catholic Church has never assumed this praxis. She holds faithfully to the uniqueness and indissolubility of matrimony, and this is a great value for all—for the family, for the children, and for the couple itself—which must be firmly maintained, faithful to Jesus' words: "What God has joined together, let no one separate" (Matt 19:6).

I can offer you no simple solution, no recipe for the innumerable cases of divorce and new marriages. But I recommend that you follow the preceding five points as a way toward conversion and reconciliation. And this call to conversion concerns us all. May our dealings with those whose marriage has failed be guided by the word of Christ: "Let anyone among you who is without sin be the first to throw a stone" (John 8:7).

9

THE SIXTH COMMANDMENT TODAY

Orientation for a Successful Marriage

GEORGE AUGUSTIN

You shall not commit adultery. Deut 5:18

✍

AN ANCIENT THEME OF HUMANITY

Today there is more or less a social agreement about the importance of the majority of the Ten Commandments, even among those for whom religion has ceased to have any relevance to daily life. But concerning the existential significance of the Sixth Commandment—the prohibition of adultery—feelings are passionately divided.

The doctrine of the Church on marriage and family, which takes this commandment as an essential reference, is considered by some as something out of date and at odds with reality. To separate sexuality from the integral realization of life, as is to some extent expounded today, creates obstacles and impediments for the formation of stable and consistent conjugal communities. The search for sexual freedom has brought with it new lacks of freedom. Emancipated sexuality foments a consumer mentality without the disposition to assume the corresponding responsibility. Furthermore, matrimonial failure and divorce are considered and accepted as fatal—sad but inevitable. In this situation it is not easy to make people understand the profound significance of the Sixth Commandment.

The present rejection of the commandment is illustrated in a somewhat familiar joke: It is said that, on descending from Sinai after receiving the Ten Commandments, Moses told his people, "I've got good news and bad. The good: I was able to bargain him down to ten. The bad: adultery won't be permitted in the future either."

Experience demonstrates that (notwithstanding the social acceptance of divorce) the conflicts and difficulties that continually arise in couples are by no means thereby resolved. Everyone knows how much suffering can come, both for parents and children, from a broken relationship. This common experience can give a glimpse of the necessity and currency of the Sixth Commandment.

The fact that this commandment forms part of the minimum demands of the Decalogue signifies that marriage and sexuality are a difficult issue not only for present society, but that they are also a most ancient theme of humanity. Despite cultural differences, people have always coincided in sensible ordering and universally binding precepts for all sexual matters as necessary for coexistence in society.

In many cultures today marriage has taken on, in contrast with previous epochs, a private, intimate, and individual character. With this, the attitude respecting the prohibition of adultery has also been modified. The traditional norms of sexual conduct are questioned extensively in public opinion.

Even though, on the one hand, a certain relativity regarding sexuality has disseminated, on the other, there is a noticeable increase of sensitivity toward the violations of feeling and love, toward infidelity and guilt.

In regard to marriage as a durable institution, it must be pointed out that the satisfactory individual configuration of life is valued more, by far, than the maintenance of a marriage with problems. At the same time many people show comprehension for the institution and social order of matrimony and family as a personal orientation, offering protection from the egotism that endangers coexistence.

If we wish to face this challenge from a Christian viewpoint, we must perceive people in their sexuality and in their sexual behavior, with its light and its darkness, and transmit to them the feeling that what matters to the Church are not prohibitions, but orientations that serve life and favor love. The profound sense of this commandment and the intention of the Church are not understood if her doctrine is considered either from the angle of a decrepit and sexophobic rigorism, or from that of a relativist laxity from the time of the so-called sexual revolution.

The point of departure for understanding the person of today could be the experiential reality that is often hidden in intimacy and silenced from embarrassment, being that it is decisive in life and in action: the motive of an insatiable anxiety for perpetual and unconditional faithfulness, coupled with the motive that gives wings to pure love. Against this background, the intention and reason for being of the Sixth Commandment take life as promise of God. At the center of the Christian message are the unconditional salvational will of God and his saving benevolence, which precede all action and faith of the person, and with which these begin to become possible. Christian existence is, for this reason, the answer that confides in the encouraging promise of God. The deep meaning of the Sixth Commandment is understood only in the framework of a sustained relationship lived with God, and only within this relationship can its permanent validity be explained. The commandments of God were given originally to us human beings in the context of liberation and salvation of the chosen people, to guarantee and make possible for them a free life.

THE BIBLICAL IDEA OF ADULTERY

The Sixth Commandment, to be understood in its function at the service of life, must be read in the framework and context of the entire Decalogue. The preamble of the Ten Commandments says, "I am the LORD, your God, who brought you out of the land of Egypt, out of the house of slavery" (Exod 20:2). Here, the decisive role is played by the name of God, YHWH, his being-for his people and his saving will to make possible a life in freedom for this people. The promulgation of the commandments is done recalling the revelation of the name of God, YHWH: "I AM WHO I AM" (Exod 3:14). In this context, the commandments are under a sign of experience of freedom. They are precepts of the God who dispenses salvation and benevolence to humans, who is interested that human life be fulfilled in his gratuitous will to make it possible. Before any merit of the people is the initiative of God. In this originating context, the objective of the Sixth Commandment is primarily to assure the life of the neighbor and his family in the society of that time. The commandment acquires its transcendence especially in connection with the Ninth Commandment, the prohibition of greed.

Adultery, in the Old Testament, is not considered a private matter. The Sixth Commandment prohibits men from breaking into another marriage. Relations with a married woman or, given the case, with a legitimately engaged woman are prohibited. The reach of the defense of the matrimony of the neighbor here intended is intelligible only in the context of the vitally necessary function and importance of the family in the society of that time.

At stake in adultery were the legitimacy of the descendents, the maintenance of the family and its property. Given that adultery threatened to make contingent in a fully real way the basis of the neighbor's life, adultery was a question of life or death (Lev 20:20; Deut 22:22ff).

The prohibited action has widespread consequences, both for the implicated and for the society as a whole, which attack seriously the freedom and the protection of the security given by God. Originally, then, the Sixth Commandment serves the protection of marriage and family; it does not directly affect other sexual infractions or sins. Nor does this commandment in the Old Testament prohibit divorce.

In the New Testament, conversely, Jesus Christ radicalized the Sixth Commandment in an unheard-of way, fixing the commencement of adultery already in intimate thoughts, looks, and desires. In the Sermon on the Mount he declares outright to the disciples, "You have heard that it was said, 'You shall not commit adultery.' But I say to you that everyone who looks at a woman with lust has already committed adultery with her in his heart." (Matt 5:27–28). But Jesus exacerbated in yet another way the prohibition of adultery, to wit, rejecting all divorce. To the question of the Pharisees in this respect, he responds, "Then in the house the disciples asked him again about this matter. He said to them, 'Whoever divorces his wife and marries another commits adultery against her; and if she divorces her husband and marries another, she commits adultery'" (Mark 10:11–12). With this he derogates the old Jewish praxis of divorce and refers on this point to the originating will of the Creator: "But from the beginning of creation, 'God made them male and female.' 'For this reason a man shall leave his father and mother and be joined to his wife, and the two shall become one flesh.' So they are no longer two, but one flesh. Therefore what God has joined together, let no one separate" (Mark 10:6–9). Matrimony is, in keeping with the will of the Creator, a community for life. Whoever wishes to explain the Ten Commandments today in accordance with the attitude of Jesus cannot dispense with his words, unequivocal in all their radicalness.

LIBERATION FOR TRUE FREEDOM

What is said about all the commandments applies especially to the Sixth: it is not a legalistic limitation of life, but a promise of God and orientation to profound liberty and human perfection. Courage and security in the future that God makes possible set the tone.

On the way from the land of slavery to the land of freedom, the commandments of God offer an inestimable point of orientation. Their updating, modified by Jesus of Nazareth, has confirmed this at a new level, that of grace. The God who wants *to be-there-for* human beings is the intimate mystery and the basic foundation for the possibility of human community.

He wants the community of life and love of woman and man to be achieved. God wants to keep his intention alive in favor of humans. "Attention! Your community of life and love is sacred, it is under my special protection. Your love is wrapped in my love and protected in it. Your mutual love is the experience of my love." The shaping force of this promise consists in the sharpening of the awareness of responsibility of one to—and for—the other. In this way, the Sixth Commandment serves as orientation for forming the conscience responsibly and for following it with the strength of God, because sexuality has a lofty symbolic character of the supreme possibility of human beings: their capacity to form community in general.

This promise, as precept of God, has its ultimate roots in faith in the gift of God. The foundation and base is faith in God. This faith is not burden, but liberation. Only in the framework of this relationship of faith and of this union of confidence in God can the person perceive the full import of this commandment. For this reason it is also of vital importance for marriage and family to revitalize the faith, deepen it, and be open to its living force.

EMPOWERMENT FOR IRREVOCABLE LOVE AND FIDELITY

This commandment is the proof of the confidence of God in human beings: you are capable of an unbreakable love. The conjugal community, as the unbreakable and exclusive mutual self-surrender of two people, is the most intense form of human community. Upon it rests the promise of God: human beings are capable of accepting and receiving each other without hurting each other. The instant is not the decisive point, says this promise; the profound desire of life in firm love and the dream of eternal fidelity: this is decisive.

Certainly, in a time that not only suffers, but that experiences the instability of change, even personal relationships like marriage run the risk of seeing themselves dragged down by the undertow of the short-term as principle.

In faithfulness, on the contrary, it's a matter of past and future: it looks back with gratitude, to the promises made and to the duties taken on; it keeps alive the memory of what was promised and anticipates a fulfilling future when it acquires commitments. It is often loss of memory of the past, as well as lack of confidence in the future, that make faithfulness vacillate. This affects even the celebration of the wedding, which is the public manifestation of fidelity.

Matrimony, as the most intimate personal community of life, is ordered fundamentally to duration. The community of love of the spouses, which encompasses the whole life, excludes any insertion of a third in the conjugal community. The desire for uniqueness and exclusivity comes tragically to the fore when one of the spouses is deceived and wounded. The community of life of the spouses, which is based on mutual fidelity and sanctified in a special manner by the sacrament of Christ, signifies indissoluble faithfulness that, in joy and sorrow, encompasses body and soul. For this reason, this community of life is particularly incompatible with all adultery.

When we speak of the sacramentality of matrimony, we speak of a stable human-divine relationship in marriage. It is of great importance that we be aware of the meaning and grace of the sacraments. The sacraments establish a mutual relation between God and people and make it possible that these latter participate in divine life. They are the visible signs of invisible grace. The sacraments must not be considered as a one-time action in a crucial moment of life, but as a new dynamic relationship with God that intensifies and reenforces with grace a vital decision by matrimony. The decision to follow Christ throughout the entire life of the marriage is an integral part of marriage itself, because the sacrament is not a simple liturgical action, but a process, a long road that demands all the faculties of the person: understanding, will, sensitivity. The reception of the sacrament is only the beginning of a dynamic life-long relationship with God. In the beginning of the itinerary of life and faith, God acts. This beginning is the basis and the point of departure on the way with God for the entire life. The action of God in the sacrament has to have an effect in the faith and life of the person. Growth on the way of faith, that is, the existential realization of that which has taken place in the sacrament is, in turn, only possible by the lasting action of the grace of God. The grace of God accompanies the initiated itinerary of life and faith, and only by its force can the marriage develop fully. The grace given in the sacraments determines, imprints, and creatively accompanies this life itinerary of the spouses.

This community on the way, propelled by grace, not only seeks to be received newly every day as gift, but is a constant call to get outside of and to surrender oneself. One transcends oneself in one's essence in a "going forward" toward God, and the human being "goes forward" toward God in the human being. At bottom, it's a call and an equipping for service to

God and to the human person. This human-divine community on the way is marriage lived in the impulse of grace. Therefore, the reception of the sacrament of matrimony is not to be understood as just a special culminating point on life's road, but rather as a point of departure for an evangelizing-mystagogic itinerary of life. It has to be understood that, step by step, we grow in the sacred within this community and, in this process, at the same time grow also in the mystery of a life that is now always present before God.

If we understand marriage as a personal community, we can understand "adultery" not only as sexual contact with a third person. Marriage is threatened by diverse injuries to the desired and hoped-for fidelity. If really, through mutual and unconditional love, the equal personal dignity of both man and woman is recognized, then the profound disappointment and hurt occasioned by adultery also becomes totally comprehensible. Here, how the wounds are handled is decisive: in the strength of God is found the disposition to forgive and, with his help, to jointly set out on a new beginning.

The experience with engaged couples in the preparation for marriage clearly demonstrates that the desire for fidelity in the matrimonial community holds a high rank in the scale of values. The couple has the firm will and the intimate desire that the matrimonial community last the entire life, because otherwise they couldn't give their *I do* to "until death does us part." The majority of married people perceive unfaithfulness in the marriage as a personal outrage and a disregard for human dignity, because love and sexuality lived exclusively cannot be separated one from the other—that is, if justice is to be done to the integrity and dignity of the human person.

From this point of view, the conjugal community faces a permanent task. With the efforts of the whole intelligence and imagination, the shaping of the relationship has to be worked out in such a way that even the thought of adultery must appear as "beneath us."

There is a lack of fidelity that without scruples abandons the companion when emotional interest wanes. Against this kind of infidelity, the resistance offered by Christian testimony experienced in conjugal faithfulness will never be excessive.

"AT THE LIMIT"—A PLACE FOR EXISTENTIAL EXPERIENCE OF FAITH

A Christianly formed marital life, along with many lovely experiences, can also bring difficulties and become almost unbearable. The conjugal community of woman and man is, evidently, a community-on-the-way, capable of evolution, which can be fulfilling, but also rocky and fragile.

Human existence, including matrimony, hardly ever transpires without faults. Marriage is not assured against human failure. Neither can the success of the marriage be guaranteed, nor can any risk be excluded.

Behind the failure or frustration of a marriage lie individual and social-psychological reasons. A failed marriage obviously brings anxious uncertainty and infinite suffering. Such at-the-limit experiences can be changed, for the believer, into existential situations of experiencing faith, without falling apart as a person in the failure of the marriage. The experience of the cross, as a place to experience God, also forms part of being Christian. For believing people God can write straight with crooked lines.

In crises, the marvel of the Holy Spirit can also be experienced as saving light and warmth that unexpectedly and gratifyingly inundates and fills with new life, because the meaning of the cross is moving on to a fullness of life that already commences here in the daily experiences of profound happiness.

The possibility of marital failure and getting rid of this painful experience—the divorce and new marriages of our time—should not, in any case, divert attention from the successful and fulfilling marriage. It is not right to lose sight of the many well and even happily married people who live their marriage with joy, believingly, and also with great strength of faith confront their crises.

The aim of the Christian message is to enable people and to encourage them to share their life as man and woman in Christian freedom, to find in the community of the whole life—whole not only as duration, but also as wholeness of life—their human fulfillment and full happiness.

If the Sixth Commandment is understood as an aid and support for the formation of conscience and an ethical task to be accomplished as a consequence of faith, today it can still provide help and perspective. This commandment can sharpen the eye to see true humanism and unmask the false.

The promise of this commandment is the full humanity, lived in faith, of the relationship between man and woman. The promise contains no tables of prohibitions and sanctions, but the true humanization and liberation of sexuality for a life in plenitude. It encourages the truly grand possibilities of human encounter. In the midst of all the problems of sexual behavior, this promise brings strength and courage, in God's name, to find true love and lifelong faithfulness.

COURAGE TO LOVE:
TRUSTING IN THE GRACE OF GOD

Love, considered biblically, is not just a feeling, but a decision of the will and of the heart for God and mankind. The decision of the heart is realized in thinking, speaking, and doing. It is a question here, above all, of doing justice to God and to mankind. There cannot be true love without justice: "Owe no one anything, except to love one another.... The commandments, "You shall not commit adultery..." and any other commandment, are summed up in this word, "Love your neighbor as yourself." Love does no wrong to a neighbor; therefore, love is the fulfilling of the law" (Rom 13:8–10). This love is concentrated irrevocably, on God's part, in the sacramentality of matrimony.

With the reception of the sacrament is expressed that the human community of love is, finally, only possible on the horizon of the grace of God. The sacrament of marriage is expression of the fidelity of God, who, in the difficult ambivalence of human love, provides support and strength. Faith that the imperfect personal existence and the conjugal relationship are grafted into the horizon of God's benevolence will help to remove expectation of perfection in oneself or in the couple and find, rather, the strength to accept the fragmentariness of one's own as well as the spouse's life, and to handle it. In this respect it is important to always reassure the intuited reality from its reference to God, so as to be able to reconcile with the not-experienced possibilities of life and with its deficiencies.

The significance of the Sixth Commandment is none other, in this context, than the realization of love and justice in the community of love and life of man and woman. In this commandment comes clearly to light, above all, the deepest desire of the person: the desire for uniqueness and singularity, to be affirmed and confirmed as a person; the desire to belong totally to one sole person and the disposition for total surrender to the other.

Seen in a purely human way, this undertaking of the spouses seems to us an enormous demand—namely, the search for plenitude in the impossible plenitude. Nonetheless, the believer can confide that God stands by his word, that which the Apostle formulated full of confidence: "My grace is sufficient for you, for power is made perfect in weakness" (2 Cor 12:9).

10

MATRIMONY

True and Proper Sacrament of the New Alliance

GERHARD LUDWIG MÜLLER

∽

THE ONTOLOGY OF THE SYMBOL AND THE CRISIS OF SACRAMENTALITY

The sacramental principle is in our days passing through a far-reaching crisis, which affects in a special way the sacramentality of marriage (cf. *DH* 1799). This crisis is the expression of the deep-seated inability of modern man to understand symbolically the overall reality of life, which refers to transcendence and offers access to it. It is caused furthermore by a mechanistic vision of the world, which considers matter exclusively from the criterion of quantity and approaches concrete and particular things thinking only of their function. As a consequence, the human being no longer sees the material world and concrete things as means to help him recognize his relation to the global horizon and the foundation of all being. When it is no longer possible to understand a materially structured symbol as means and expression of the transcendent reality, the sacraments also become unthinkable. The theology of the sacraments likewise depends on a philosophical-ontological clarification as foundation upon which are built all the other ways of access to the symbol, in all of its aspects.

A symbol is not an arbitrarily constructed system, torn away from the rest of reality. Instead, reality must be understood symbolically in its universal structure: being, as general actuality of the particular entity, is expressed in this latter; entity is self-expression of being, which does not exist independently from it. The entity is limited to expressing the totality of being as a fragment, in keeping with its limiting essence, of the general actuality of being. Hence the world, in its existence, is capable of being the symbol in which is manifest "the eternal power and divinity of God," that is, the symbol in which these "are made accessible to reason by the creatures" (cf. Rom 1:20; Acts 17:24; Wis 13:1–9; Sir 17:8ff). The "symbolic of being" (*Seinssymbolik*) considers, then, the entity "for itself": the entity has symbolic character insofar as it presents and expresses, in determined attributes and features, something distinct from itself—for example, the spiritual in the material, the soul in the body, or, better put, the soul as body.

THE HUMAN BODY:
THE ORIGINATING SYMBOL

As all other beings, man is called into existence by God, which doesn't exclude that he, by virtue of his spiritual nature, possesses his own real causality, which is given him to own (*causa formalis*) and allows him to personally fulfill himself and to express himself consequently with eschatological dynamic in the natural conditions of his corporal-spiritual essence in history and society. His corporal-spiritual nature becomes the dynamic foundation of his possibility to communicate in fact with himself and to be personally in others in his being. This act is the human being. He is not in the first place in himself a pure spirit who later, in a second moment, communicates with himself and goes out to meet other people. Self-expression in matter and interpersonal communication in its material corporality represent the essential constitutive factor of the personal spirit and the freedom of man. The bodily-spiritual constitution of human beings and their binary sexuality are natural conditions for "becoming *una caro* (one flesh)" and for rendering sacramental the natural marital bond between man and woman.

Another concept related to this self-expression is that of the "body." The body is the real symbol (*Realsymbol*) of the soul. The body is but the actuality of the soul itself in its expression in the *raw material*, that is, the pure possibility through which it manifests and acts. Thus, corporality does not erect an obstacle between two souls who want to move toward one another; rather, it makes possible, supports, and conditions the interpersonal encounter.

Not even does the personal and direct relationship with God takes place outside of the given conditions of human existence, but rather within them. A personal and direct relationship in a merely spiritual environment that transcends created nature turns out to be impossible for the human being. Only God is situated in a pure and direct relation with God. Since the Word of God has become man, it is possible for the human being to establish a personal and direct relationship with God through the personal meeting with the man Jesus and communion in the community of his disciples; moreover, such relationship with God has as an inseparable factor (founded in the theology of the creation and confirmed by the incarnation) this mediated structure.

Part of the definition of the human being is his relation with time and space. This reference belongs, as just explained, in an altogether specific way to his bodily-spiritual self-expression. To be more exact, it characterizes his symbolic self-realization against the background of history and society. Hence, the human being can be reached and determined by a past or future action of God, historically mediated and with a view to society; in effect, he can be made participant in such an event, especially through the pertinent symbols. But this supposes at the same time that this acting of God has to occur in a human mediator. Otherwise, the universal communication and mediation of the unique and unrepeatable action (or event) of God would not have symbolic form.

Because of this, the man Jesus Christ (cf. 1 Tim 2:5), mediator of the Kingdom of God, can make human beings participants in his saving acting in history through symbols and words, gestures and actions; more exactly, through the real memory of this action consummated in the past and through the symbolic act that actualizes and anticipates the future promise, that is, the full eschatological realization of the redemption effectuated by means of the past historical fact.

THE DIVERSITY OF SYMBOLS IN THE LIFE OF THE HUMAN BEING

A human being's own biography never seems foreign to him. It is a temporally structured self-expression through which is reached the overall actuality of his persona. In all biographies there are special happenings that are converted into key symbols and turning points of human existence.

Conception and birth are also, besides the positive aspects of the events, symbols of the beginning of a finite spirit in the world and contain, consequently, a natural symbolic dimension, which refers to the absolute origin of the human being in God (cf. baptism). Personal growth is the natural symbol of the temporal structure, the historical nature, and the way of man toward his consummation. Hence the symbolic representation of birth and maturation may be converted into the symbolic expression of the fact that the Christian travels his vital path in the force of the Holy Spirit who strengthens him (cf. confirmation). The ingestion of food by the human being is the fundamental symbol of the permanent maintenance of vital force and makes food the symbol of this vital force, of the constitutive relation of man with matter. Thus all food already contains a natural symbolism that refers to the absolute sense in which each person receives his own life from God, Author of life (cf. Eucharist).

By virtue of its historical and social constitution, the primordial symbol of the body is displayed in determined concretions, which for their part can convert into symbolic nodal points of human communication with God and of God with human beings. Only thanks to the fact that the putting into practice of human existence is symbolic can God convert it into the center of interpersonal communication. The Christian liturgy and the sacraments are not the expression of an initiative assumed by the human being to obtain something from God or to win his favor. The Christian cult of God presupposes the reconciliation of the human being with God that God himself has already effected (cf. 2 Cor 5:20), and is the symbolic celebration of the communion with God that is conceded to man in the new alliance. In the liturgy is realized the participation in the giving of oneself to the Father through Jesus and in the communion with him in the Holy Spirit (cf. Gal 4:4–6; 1 Cor 10:16ff; 11:24ff).

THE SACRAMENT OF MATRIMONY

Likewise, Christian marriage is expression of the sacramentality of grace in the Church and, therefore, one of the "seven sacraments of the new alliance" (*DH* 1800; 1891). By "Christian marriage" is understood the lifelong community, chosen integrally, exclusively, and personally between two baptized, one sole man and one sole woman, which reflects the alliance of Christ with his Church, by virtue of which the marriage becomes effective sign of the transmission of sanctifying grace.

Dogmatics considers Christian marriage from the formal aspect of sacramentality and the essential characteristics derived therefrom, such as indissolubility, monogamy, and fecundity, this last associated with the disposition to receive and educate children and to be the first witnesses of the faith for them. Moral theology deals with matrimony from the viewpoint of the anthropology of sexuality and responsible parenthood. Canon law studies matrimony in the light of its legal realization, matrimonial impediments, and so on. Pastoral theology approaches it moved by the desire to promote it and favor its success and keeps in mind the challenge of carrying out a pastoral activity for the divorced faithful, both for those who have remarried and those who haven't, in consonance with the situation. But matrimony is also a subject of civil law and of the human and social sciences.

In the bull of union for the Armenians of the Council of Ferrara-Florence (1439), matrimony is described in the categories of patristic and scholastic sacramentology, following Ephesians 5:32 as "sign of the union of Christ and the Church" (cf. *DH* 1327). Since, unlike what occurs in the other sacraments, the category of human minister of the sacrament—that is, the bride and groom themselves or the celebrating priest—can hardly be applied to matrimony, the Florentine council limited itself to speaking of the efficient cause of the sacrament, stemming from the *I do*, in the consent of the bride and groom. In its intrinsic supernatural reality, marriage includes three goods: 1) the *bonum prolis*, the good of the offspring, of the descendents, that is, the acceptance of the children and the willingness to educate them such that they recognize God and serve him; 2) the *bonum fidei*, that is, the good of reciprocal, exclusive, and lifelong fidelity; 3) the *bonum sacramenti*, which is the good of the indissolubility and indestructibility of the sacramental bond, which has permanent fundament in the indivisible unity between Christ and the Church, made visible in matrimony. Even though a temporally limited or unlimited interruption of the physical community of life, the separation of "table and bed" so to speak, can be possible, "it is not licit to enter into another marriage, since the bond of legitimately contracted matrimony is perpetual" (*DH* 1327). The marital bond between both spouses, indissoluble in life, corresponds in a certain sense with the seal (*res et sacramentum*) impressed in baptism, confirmation, and the sacrament of ordination.

Current theology views matrimony especially in an ecclesiological context. In light of a personal and communicative anthropology of greater breadth, Vatican II describes it as one of the fundamental sacramental acts of the Church:

> Finally, Christian spouses, by virtue of the sacrament of matrimony, by which they signify and participate in the mystery of unity and fertile love between Christ and the Church (cf. Ep 5,32), mutually help each other to sanctify themselves in conjugal life and in the procreation and education of the offspring, and thereby possess their own gift, within the people of God, in their state and form of life (cf. 1 Co 7,7). From this consort proceeds the family, in which new citizens of human society are born, who, by the grace of the Holy Spirit, are constituted children of God in baptism, who perpetuate throughout time the people of God. In this kind of domestic Church the parents should be the first preachers of faith, through word and example, to their children and should foment the vocation proper to each one, but with special care the sacred vocation. (*LG* 11)

BIBLICAL TESTIMONY OF MATRIMONY

Now it is necessary to go deeper into the biblical considerations concerning marriage. In the Old Testament narrations of the creation, the authors go beyond the concrete matrimonial praxis of the epoch and take as reference the originating will of the Creator and the order of creation not yet sullied by sin: they question or see as relative on principle the patriarchal understanding of the man and woman, as well as the customary polygamy, the basic possibility of divorce, and the possibility to repudiate the spouse.

The Yahwistic narration of the creation stresses the egalitarian and personal relation between the man and the woman. Only the woman proceeding from Adam, taken from him, can be his equal and, hence, a personal life companion in the context of mutual "help." Genesis 2:24 does not speak, in effect, of a slave, but of the intrasubjective relation of the person as principle of his perfecting. The man, who recognizes in the woman the same human nature and personal equality ("flesh of my flesh"), leaves his family of origin and thus unites with his woman, so as to be with her "one flesh, *una caro*," that is, to found a community of life in love (cf. Gen 2:24).

The priestly narrative of the creation affirms that human nature, both masculine and feminine, is created in the likeness and image of God. The intracreatural relationship between man and woman is, because of this, sign of the relationship of all creatures with God. To the man and the woman—and to the personal community that they form—are entrusted the gifts and tasks of fecundity, as well as the utlilization of the earth and the responsibility for the world. This community of man and woman is situated under the blessing and the word of the divine promise (cf. Gen 1:27ff).

From the late writings of the Old Testament is gleaned that the blessing of God (*eulogia*) on the personal love between man and woman is reflected in the thanksgiving (*eucharistia*) of the human being to God for the gift of marriage and conjugal life, whose finality is to glorify God (cf. Tob 8:4–9). Marriage was not established in its origin as a merely natural order. As already suggested, as created reality it was a symbolic allusion to the origin of the human being in God and at the same time a means through which God communicated his blessing to creation. As community of human life, marriage represented symbolically the communion of divine and human life and, more concretely, the originating unity between nature and grace, between creation and alliance. After the loss of the originating communion with God, marriage also fell under the influence and burden of the loss of grace, as underlined by the "curse" pronounced over the man and the woman (cf. Gen 2:25—3:24).

In the New Testament, marriage is situated in the historical-salvational process of the redemption of the human being, as well as in the reestablishment of the originating unity between alliance and creation, between grace and nature. In light of the salvational event of Christ, the originating determination of marriage is again underlined. This is characterized most inwardly by the new alliance of God with his people; it is no coincidence that the alliance of God with Israel was presented symbolically as a relationship of love between spouses (or bride and groom; cf. Mal 2:14; Prov 2:17). The lack of faith and the rupture of the alliance on the part of the people were stigmatized as adultery (cf. Exod 20:14; Hos 1:2). The Church as people of the new alliance has her origin in the loving surrender of Christ on the cross: Christ is her bridegroom, just as the third chapter of the Gospel of John emphasizes, "He who has the bride is the bridegroom" (John 3:29). Hence the love between man and woman, by virtue of which marriage exists, has its origin in this self-oblation of Jesus for his Church, which she represents and with which she is profoundly filled (cf. Eph 5:21, 33: 2 Cor 11:2; Rev 19:7); the Church is the bride who prepares for the wedding with the Lamb, with Christ, author and mediator of the new alliance. Finally, the author of the Letter to the Ephesians considers that the community of life of man and woman is founded on the mutual relation of "love" (*agápe*) of husband and wife and on the "obedience" of the wife to the husband. In Christianity, "obedience" must always be conceived christologically, differentiated from sociologically understood submission. Thus, Paul can classify this community of life as profound mystery (*mysterion/sacramentum magnum*), which he sets in relationship with Christ and his Church (cf. Eph 5,32).

The prepaschal Jesus places marriage in his proclamation of the kingdom of God. With this he transcends the matrimonial casuistry of the pragmatic regulations of divorce inasmuch as he refers to the originating order of creation, in which is made manifest the saving plan of God. Such regulations, according to which the man could abandon and repudiate the woman, were mere concessions made due to the "hard-heartedness" of the Israelites, which Moses and the scribes of the old alliance had tolerated, though never approved, since "at the beginning of the creation it wasn't like that." The man and the woman become definitively one, no longer two: "Therefore what God has joined together, let no one separate" (Mark 10:6–9; cf. Matt 19:1–9).

Therefore, Jesus doesn't conceive the fact of marriage as a neutral institution in the perspective of salvation or as a secondary field of lived Christian morality. Marriage is the originating form of the encounter with God and his salvational plan, because of which Jesus can make indissoluble matrimony as personal community of life a sign of the coming kingdom of God, of the kingdom of God that has taken on reality and become effective. Here the ethics of matrimony has its foundation.

The man who abandons and repudiates his wife or the woman who abandons and repudiates her husband "commit adultery" and thus infringe upon "the new alliance" (cf. Mark 10:11; Luke 16:18; 1 Cor 7:10). This fundamental intention of Jesus is not rendered ineffective by the secondary "lust clauses" (cf. Matt 5:32; 19:9), according to which separation is possible in the case of adultery. Nor is it annulled by the *privilegium paulinum* of 1 Corinthians 7:15ff, which allows converts to Christianity to abandon their still pagan spouses if these do not desire to live in peace together. Paul does not offer a precise answer to the question of to what degree it is licit for the converted spouse to wed a second time. The human being is not equipped to deal with the demands of the indissolubility of marriage as sign of the new and eternal alliance merely from his own moral forces and personal disposition. Only by accepting the call to conversion, to faith, and to follow Christ (cf. Mark 1:15), and to life in the strength of the Holy Spirit (cf. Gal 5:25), can he personally fulfill the interior reality of marriage as sign of the communion and alliance of Christ with the Church. The spiritual and corporal communion between man and woman is called to be sacred and is set upon sanctification through the Holy Spirit (cf. 1 Thess 4:3–8).

But since marriage is also situated in the context of the kingdom of God, it must be affirmed that in the human form of life, it likewise belongs to the provisional time of this world and, as we now know it, will no longer exist in the future world (cf. Mark 12:25). That's why it is licit to enter into a new marriage after the death of a spouse. The personal vocation to put oneself at the service of the arrival of the kingdom of God, on the one hand, and the call of Jesus (cf. 1 Cor 7:7), on the other, may lead, as in the case of Jesus, to a life in which matrimony is no longer a goal, but that one instead follows the "call of God" (cf. 1 Cor 7:17; cf. Luke 14:20) and, with the aid of the supernatural gift (*charisma*) of celibate life, consecrates oneself entirely to the "Lord's cause" (cf. 1 Cor 7:32).

According to St. Paul, each person and each Christian is free to opt in a completely personal manner, in light of the salvational context of matrimony, for the form of life naturally most adequate for him or her (cf. 1 Cor 7:7, 28, 38, 40; Matt 19:12). But once the man and the woman are married he exhorts them, "To the married I give this command—not I but the Lord—that the wife should not separate from her husband (but if she does separate, let her remain unmarried or else be reconciled to her husband), and that the husband should not divorce his wife" (1 Cor 7:10–11). Marriage between Christians, consecrated in Jesus Christ (cf. 1 Cor 7:39), is entered into and lived "in the Lord" (1 Cor 1:2). Paul also testifies in this way to a supernatural theological dimension of marriage founded christologically. Against all contempt on the part of the Gnostic heretics, who aim to prohibit matrimony (cf. 1 Tim 4:4), he highlights the participation of marriage in the goodness of all creation. A marriage lived in mutual fidelity is in keeping with the will of God and "Let marriage be held in honor by all" (Heb 13:4).

Although the "codes of domestic duties" (*Haustasfeln*) suggest a certain subordination of the wife to the husband (cf. Col 3:18; Eph 5:23–33; 1 Pet 3:1–7), that does not permit the drawing of any conclusion in the sense of a religious sanction of determined social conditions. Such texts speak rather of a reciprocal subordination "out of reverence for Christ" (Eph 5:21), who, in the obedience of his love, is God's model of the communion of life with his people. An altruistic attitude may win over nonbelieving spouses to the word of the gospel; by the "purity and reverence of [their] lives" wives can attract their husbands to the faith even without words (cf. 1 Pet 3:2; cf. 1 Cor 7:14).

THE THEOLOGY OF THE ALLIANCE AND THE SACRAMENT OF MATRIMONY

Referring to modern anthropology, Vatican II proposes a more personalistic conception of marriage. This leads it to reconsider the doctrine of the "hierarchy of the ends of marriage" in the form extant until then. The Council tried to clarify the integral relation between personal love, openness to the gift of fecundity, and responsibility toward the children. The Council is fully aware of the worsening of conditions for a successful marital and family life in modern society, characterized by the dissolution of—and the fear of—lasting bonds, the notion of sexuality as means of self-satisfaction apart from a lasting relationship, and so on (cf. *GS* 47). In view of the shattering increase in the number of divorces, the demand for a necessary pastoral program for divorced faithful, both for those who have civilly remarried and those who haven't, is heard with growing intensity.

From the perspective of dogmatic theology, a systematic point of departure is important: the Council situates the sacrament of matrimony in the context of a theology of the alliance and confirms first of all the classical doctrine of marriage. Marriage is born concretely from a free and personal act in which the bride and groom give themselves to and are accepted by each other. Thus they enter into the form of life of the matrimonial community, which, in accordance with divine stipulation, exists as a permanent institution. Hence marriage is not now subject exclusively to human will: "God himself is the author of matrimony, to which he has given diverse goods and ends" (*GS* 48). Matrimony is of capital importance for the survival of humanity, for the personal development of the distinct members of the family, and for their salvation. Marriage and family contribute to the humanization of the person and of the whole society. Conjugal love is ordered to the acceptance of life and the education of the children. At the same time, matrimony is an alliance between man and woman that includes a personal communion of life and unconditional faithfulness.

It is worth reproducing at length the central paragraph of number 48 of the pastoral constitution *Gaudium et spes*:

Christ our Lord blessed abundantly this multiform love, born from the divine source of charity and which is formed in likeness to his union with the Church. Because as God in antiquity came forward to unite with his people in an alliance of love and fidelity (cf. Ho 2; Jr 3, 6–13; Ezk 16,23; Is 54), so now the Savior of mankind and the Spouse of the Church (cf. Mt 9,15; Mk 2, 19–20; Lk 5, 34–35; Jn 3,29; 2 Co 11,2; Ep 5,27; Rv 19,7–8; 21,2.9) comes to meet the Christian spouses in the sacrament of matrimony. Furthermore, he remains with them so that the spouses, in their mutual surrender, love each other with perpetual fidelity, as he himself loved the Church and surrendered himself for her (cf. Ep 5,25). Genuine conjugal love is assumed in the divine love and is governed and enriched by the redemptive virtue of Christ and the salvational action of the Church to lead effectively the spouses to God and aid and fortify them in the sublime mission of paternity and maternity (cf. LG 15–16, 40–41 and 47). By this the Christian spouses, in order to fulfill worthily their duties of state, are strengthened and as consecrated by a special sacrament (cf. Pious XI, Enc. *Casti connubii*, AAS 22 [1930], 583), by whose virtue, upon fulfilling their conjugal and familiar mission, imbued with the Spirit of Christ, which saturates their whole life with faith, hope and love, they arrive ever nearer to their own perfection and mutual sanctification and, therefore, jointly to the glorification of God.

ANTHROPOLOGICAL AND SACRAMENTOLOGICAL REFLECTIONS

The doctrine of the indissolubility of matrimony often encounters incomprehension in secularized environments. Where the foundations of Christian faith have been lost, a merely conventional belonging to the Church is no longer sufficient to guide the principal vital decisions and can hardly offer the needed support in the crises of the matrimonial state, and this is valid analogously for the priesthood and consecrated life. Many ask themselves, How can I link myself for life to one sole woman or one sole man? Who can tell me how things will be after ten, twenty, or thirty years of marriage? Is it possible to link oneself once and for all to one sole person?

The multiple current experiences of broken matrimonial communities reenforces even more the skepticism of young people looking at definitive vital decisions.

On the other hand, the ideal of fidelity between man and woman, founded on the order of the creation, has lost none of its attraction, as recent surveys of young people demonstrate. A majority of those polled pursue a stable and lasting vital relationship, since that corresponds to the spiritual and moral essence of the human being. Allow us to recall in addition the anthropological value of indissoluble marriage: it frees the spouses from the malice and tyranny of feelings and moods; it helps them to take on personal difficulties and overcome painful experiences; it especially protects the children, whose lot it is to suffer the greater part of the painful experiences caused by broken marriages.

Love is more than a feeling or a prepersonal instinct; in its essence, it is surrender. In conjugal love, two people tell each other in an altogether deliberate way and with total freedom, only you, and you forever. The words of the Lord, "What God has joined…", correspond to the promise of the bride and groom: "I take you as my husband…I take you as my wife. I promise to love and respect you all the days of my life, until death do us part." The priest blesses and confirms "in the Lord" the alliance that the spouses have sealed before God. The doubts as to whether the conjugal bond possesses an ontological nature dissipate in light of the word of God: "Have you not read that the one who made them at the beginning 'made them male and female,' and said, 'For this reason a man shall leave his father and mother and be joined to his wife, and the two shall become one flesh'? So they are no longer two, but one flesh. Therefore what God has joined together, let no one separate" (Matt 19:4–6).

Christians are governed by the fact that matrimony between the baptized, who have thus been incorporated into the body of Christ, has a sacramental character and constitutes, therefore, a supernatural reality, which is not given to the human being to arrange. One of the main pastoral problems at present stems from the exclusively worldly and pragmatic standpoint by which many of our contemporaries judge marriage. But whoever thinks according to the "spirit of the world" (cf. 1 Cor 2:12) is not able to comprehend the sacramentality of matrimony. The Church cannot respond to the growing lack of perception of the sacredness of marriage simply by means of a pragmatic adaptation to what seems inevitable, but must do so rather from confidence in "the Spirit that is from God, so that we may understand the gifts bestowed on us by God" (1 Cor 2:12). Sacramental marriage is a testimony to the power of grace, which transforms the person and prepares the entire Church for the Holy City, for the New Jerusalem, the Church herself, adorned "as a bride adorned for her husband" (Rev 21:2). The message of the sacredness of matrimony must be proclaimed today with prophetic frankness. A lukewarm prophet, in adapting to the spirit of the times, seeks his own redemption, not the redemption of the world in Jesus Christ. Fidelity to the matrimonial promise is a prophetic salvational sign that God concedes the world: "Let anyone accept this who can" (Matt 19:12). By means of sacramental grace conjugal love is purified, strengthened and multiplied: "This love, ratified by mutual fidelity and, above all, by the sacrament of Christ, is indissolubly faithful, in body and mind, in prosperity and adversity, and, therefore, excluded from it are all adultery and divorce" (*GS* 49). The spouses, who by virtue of the sacrament of marriage participate in the definitive and irrevocable love of God, can thus be witnesses to the faithful love of God, nourishing constantly their own love with a life of faith and love of neighbor.

Without doubt there are situations, as every shepherd of souls well knows, in which, due to grave causes, cohabitation turns out to be simply impossible, as in instances of physical and psychological violence. In these painful situations the Church has always permitted the separation of the spouses and the termination of cohabitation. It is necessary to affirm, however, that the conjugal bond of a matrimony before God continues to exist and neither of the spouses is free to enter into a new marriage while the other is alive (cf. 1 Cor 7:10–39). For this reason, Christian communities and their priests are encouraged to open in every way possible paths to reconciliation; but when this proves to be impossible, the difficult personal situation must be confronted with faith. Nor is it licit to say that the precepts of God cannot be observed due to human weakness (cf. *DH* 1568).

OBSERVATIONS OF MORAL THEOLOGY

With great repercussion in the media some affirm that a decision concerning the possible reception of eucharistic communion must be left to the personal conscience of the divorced and remarried faithful. This argument, which rests on a problematic concept of conscience, was rejected in a letter of the Congregation for the Doctrine of the Faith on the 14th of September, 1994: "Letter to the Bishops of the Catholic Church concerning the Reception of Eucharistic Communion by Divorced Faithful Who Have Remarried." It's true that the faithful are recommended to examine their conscience in every Holy Mass to determine if they are in conditions to receive the sacred communion, for which the existence of a serious fault not yet forgiven is always an impediment. They have, however, the duty to edify their conscience and orient it to the truth. All faithful are invited to listen to the authority of the Church. In the words of Pope John Paul II,

> The authority of the Church, which pronounces on moral questions, does not in any way undermine the freedom of conscience of Christians; not only because the freedom of conscience is never freedom regarding the truth, but always and only in the truth, but also because Church teaching does not present truths estranged from the Christian conscience, but manifests the truths that it should already possess, developing them from the originating act of faith. The Church puts herself only and always at the service of the conscience, helping it not to be buffeted to and fro by whatever wind of doctrine according to the deceit of men (cf. Ep 4,14), not to deviate from the truth concerning the good of mankind, but to reach with security, especially in the most difficult questions, the truth and maintain itself in it. (*Veritatis splendor* 64)

If divorced faithful who have remarried are subjectively convinced in conscience that their previous marriage is null, this must be established in objective form by the competent matrimonial tribunal, because the conscience of the individual refers to the sacramental salvational order, as does this latter to the former. Marriage concerns the relationship between two people and God, but is also a reality of the Church, a sacrament, about whose validity not only the individual alone has to decide, but also the Church, of which by baptism and confirmation he has converted into member. "If the previous marriage of faithful divorced who have remarried was valid, their new union can in no case be considered licit by the fact that for intrinsic reasons it is not fitting to restrict the reception of the sacraments. The conscience of the individual is subject without exceptions to this norm."[1] Nor applicable in this case is the doctrine of *epiqueya*, according to which a law, though having general validity, doesn't always correspond completely to human action; the indissolubility of sacramental matrimony is a norm of divine law and not subject, therefore, to the authority of the Church. In keeping with this, a second marriage is not possible while the first spouse is alive (cf. *DH* 1802, 1807). The Church possesses, however, full authority relating to the *privilegium paulinum*, that is, in the moment of establishing which conditions must be fulfilled before a marriage can be defined as indissoluble in the meaning that Jesus himself gave to this term. Concerning this foundation, the Church has defined the matrimonial impediments that render impossible the validity of the marriage and has developed the pertinent canonical procedures.

In the last instance, time and again mercy is invoked in favor of the admittance of the sacraments to the faithful divorced and remarried, given that Jesus expressed solidarity with suffering people and showed them his merciful love; hence mercy is a special sign of the authentic following of Christ. This is true; but it doesn't hold up as an argument in questions relating to the theology of the sacraments, also—and above all—because the entire sacramental order is the work of divine mercy and cannot be revoked by invoking the same principle of mercy that sustains it. Resulting from an objectively problematic appellation to mercy is incurred the danger of trivializing the image of God, in accordance with which only God can forgive. In addition to mercy, holiness and justice also form part of the mystery of God. If these divine attributes are forgotten or ignored and the reality of sin is not taken seriously, it is no longer even possible to transmit God's mercy to human beings. Jesus approached the adulteress with great empathy, but at the same time he told her: "Go your way, and from now on do not sin again" (John 8:11). The mercy of God does not obviate the divine commandments or the doctrine of the Church; on the contrary, it concedes the force of grace to observe them, to be healed after the fall, and to lead a full life in the image of the celestial Father.

FAITH AND THE SACRAMENT OF MATRIMONY

In the already cited introduction to the volume of commentaries on the letter of the Congregation for the Doctrine of the Faith concerning the reception of the eucharistic communion on the part of the faithful divorced and remarried, the then-prefect of said congregation, Cardinal Joseph Ratzinger, manifests the clearly perceived need to carry out profound clarifying studies on the relation between the real attitude of faith and marriage and its consequences for the validity of the marriage; such studies cannot be postponed any longer:

The question as to whether non-believing baptized Christians, be it that they have never believed, be it that they have lost the faith, can truly enter into valid sacramental matrimony requires new and more profound investigations. In other words, it must be clarified whether all marriage between two baptized is really ipso facto a sacramental marriage. The Code of Canonic Law also establishes that only a "valid" matrimonial contract is at the same time sacramental (cf. CIC can. 1055 sec. 2). Faith belongs to the essence of marriage; so then, it is necessary to clarify the juridical question as to what degree of "no faith" has as a consequence that a sacrament is not realized.[2]

Borrowing words from a known canonist of the 1980s, it can be affirmed that the problem stems from

> determining the degree of faith necessary for the realization of the sacrament. The classical doctrine has adopted until now a minimalist position, counting itself satisfied simply with the intention to do *quod facit ecclesia* [what the Church does]. In the present context of a Christianity in which the faith of the individual believer can no longer be automatically supposed, it appears necessary to require an explicit faith, to the end of preserving Christian matrimony from secularization.[3]

All the more timely is a reanalysis of the doctrine on the sacraments in the documents of Vatican II. The Constitution on the Church, *Lumen gentium*, in its second chapter, dedicated to the people of God, recalls the capital importance of the sacraments as constitutive elements for the Church to intrinsically interlink the universal priesthood of the faithful and the ordained priesthood in view of her mission in the world as sacrament of salvation and real sign of eternal salvation for the faithful proper.

In this mission of sanctification, the sacrament of matrimony plays a key role in the Church and in society:

> Finally, the Christian spouses, by virtue of the sacrament of matrimony, by which they signify and participate in the mystery of unity and fertile love between Christ and the Church (cf. Ep 5,32), mutually help each other to sanctify themselves in conjugal life and in the procreation and education of the offspring, and thereby posses their own gift, within the people of God, in their state and form of life (cf. 1 Co 7,7). From this consort proceeds the family, in which are born new citizens of human society, who by the grace of the Holy Spirit, are constituted in baptism children of God, who perpetuate throughout time the people of God. In this kind of domestic Church the parents should be for their children the first preachers of the faith, by means of word and example, and foment the vocation proper to each one, but with special care the sacred vocation. (*LG* 11)

Our considerations wish to serve the rediscovery of this personal gift of the sacrament of matrimony in the people of God especially, but also as individual vocation on the way toward holiness. Thus, *Lumen gentium* concludes the reflection on the sacraments as call also today with the following words: "All faithful Christians, of whatever condition and state, fortified with so many and such powerful means of salvation, are called by the Lord, each one by his own path, to the perfection of that holiness with which the Father himself is perfect" (*LG* 11).

NOTES

✍

1. THE DEVOLUTION OF AN AMERICAN CATHOLIC FAMILY

1. According to Catholic teaching, any sex outside of heterosexual marriage that is not simultaneously unitive and procreative is "gravely sinful." Premarital sex, birth control, masturbation, purely unitive sex between spouses, and all homosexual acts are condemned. Though homosexual attraction is considered acceptable, all homosexual activity is designated as "intrinsically disordered." Despite this, recent polls show 82 percent of American Catholics believe birth control is not immoral, while a clear majority favor same-sex civil marriages.

2. In May 2014, Archbishop Silvano Tomasi told a United Nations panel that 858 priests had been dismissed and an additional 2,572 members of the clergy disciplined for sexual abuse of children 2004–13. Archbishop Tomasi also stated $2.5 billion of Church funds had been paid out to some of the victims of these crimes.

3. Over time, *Mallet* became *Malette*. In 1802, my grandfather's grandfather married a Marie-Rose with no last name in Rigaud, Quebec, across from the Ottawa River, where the Mohawks resided. Though native Indian blood is clearly represented in the Malettes, Hector and his descendants are regarded as French Canadians.

4. Relatives were asked to choose their current affiliation/belief system from the following taxonomy: 1) practicing Roman Catholic; 2) nonpracticing Roman Catholic; 3) Protestant; 4) Christian;

5) Jewish; 6) spiritual; 7) agnostic; 8) atheistic; 9) Buddhist; and 10) uncertain but still looking. For those no longer living, a best estimation by those closest to them at the time of their death has been used. Divorced and converted Catholics are also indicated.

5. Frank Chauvin's brother Bob—Irene's brother-in-law—became a priest with the Basilian order. Bill grew up as a devout Catholic, involving himself deeply in the faith his grandparents and parents cherished. Over time, however, hypocritical behavior by lay- and religious people alike alienated Bill from the Church and the concept of Christianity more generally. Today, my cousin Bill Chauvin characterizes himself as agnostic, as do his wife Barb and their three sons, Mark, Jeff, and Scott.

6. Larry Keeley, in his capacity as an innovation consultant, has been hired by the Church of Jesus Christ of Latter Day Saints to help innovate. He was impressed to learn the Mormons have three satellites and hundreds of global TV and radio stations around the world, this for a faith with only 15 million followers. By contrast, the Holy See has one functioning web site and a single satellite channel for 1.2 billion adherents.

7. At this writing, the struggle to enroll Christophe Armitage in the Mary Queen of Peace School in St. Louis continues. Given that the Armitages offered to pay for all related costs their son might generate, material constraints are clearly not the issue.

8. Caroline was recently an associate at Solutions for Poverty, an NGO that seeks private/public partnership solutions for economically disadvantaged women all over the world. Sophie has taught English in Mexico for both regular and special needs students and also worked with battered women. Juliette is a recently returned volunteer for Peace Corps in Guinea, Africa, where she taught mathematics and conducted pioneering advocate work for local Muslim women.

9. Fr. Theodore Hesburgh concelebrated our wedding in Nyon, Switzerland. Saskia's father, Bernard Bory, is a descendent of William of Orange and a long line of persecuted Huguenots. Her mother

Johanna Schrofer also comes from a staunch line of Dutch Protestants. Catholics were not particularly kind to my wife's ancestors.

10. Dick writes, "As I approach the end of my life, my faith has weakened. I am not a comfortable man. My feelings on the Catholic Church are conflicted. I want to have that warm feeling I often got as a boy listening to favored nuns and priests talk about God—the security it provides, the loving father who always understands and forgives."

2. THOUGHTS ABOUT REALITY AND SACRAMENTS

1. Cf. J. Pieper, "Gibt es eine nicht-christliche Philosophie?," in *Werke*, by J. Pieper, vol. 8.1 (Hamburg, 1995), 109ff.

2. The pairs of terms, *poverty-ambition* and *obedience-egoism*, should be treated in an analogous way.

3. Cf. J. Pieper, "Schöpfung und Sakrament," in *Werke*, by J. Pieper, vol. 7 (Hamburg, 2000), 376ff.

4. Cf. W. Kasper, *The Gospel of the Family* (Sal Terrae: Santander, 2014), 88.

5. Ibid., 78.

6. Cf. G. K. Chesterton, *The Superstition of Divorce* (New York, 2009) followed by *Divorce versus Democracy* (Sevilla: Espuela de Plata, Valencina de la Concepción 2013).

7. W. Kasper, *Gospel of the Family*, 39.

8. Ibid., 40.

9. R. Spaemann, *Personen* (Stuttgart, 1998), 248ff (*People: Concerning the Distinction between "Something" and "Someone"*, [Pamplona: EUNSA, 2000]).

10. Cf. J. Ratzinger, "Die neuen Heiden und die Kirche,", *Gesammelte Schriften*, by J. Ratzinger, vol. 8.2 (Freiburg i.Br., 2010), 1148.

4. MERCY, JUSTICE, AND LAW

1. Francis X. Rocca, "Pope Calls Synod to Discuss Families, Divorce, and Remarriage," *Catholic News Service*, October 8, 2013, http://www.catholicnews.com/data/stories/cns/1304231.htm.

2. Walter Kasper, *Mercy: The Essence of the Gospel and the Key to Christian Life*, trans. William Madges (New York/Mahwah, NJ: Paulist Press, 2013), 9.

3. Ibid., 45.

4. Ibid., 55. See also p. 56: "Thus God's mercy is the power of God that sustains, protects, promotes, builds up, and creates life anew. It burst the logic of human injustice, which entails the punishment and death of the sinner. God's mercy desires life. In fidelity to the covenant with his people, God mercifully reestablishes the relationship with him that was destroyed by sin and he grants dependable living conditions anew. Mercy is God's option for life."

5. Ibid., 83. Kasper argues that mercy is a mirror of the self-communicative love of the Trinity. Ibid., 91–96.

6. Ibid., 89. Needless to say, working out the relationship of mercy and justice is extremely difficult. Justice is generally defined as giving each person her due, of respecting the moral fundamental order of the world. Yet it is also a virtue oriented toward the common good of the community. Divine mercy, one might say, is the quality by which God enables sinners to continue to exist, in a situation where justice, by itself, would call for their destruction as punishment for their sins.

7. Ibid., 97.

8. Ibid., 109.

9. Ibid., 157.

10. Pope John Paul II, *Dives in Misericordia* (1980).

11. Kasper, *Mercy*, 159.

12. Ibid., 169.

13. Ibid., 179.

14. Ibid., 177.

15. Ibid., 180.

16. Walter Kasper, *The Gospel of the Family* (New York/Mahwah, NJ: Paulist Press, 2014). This is his lecture to the Extraordinary Consistory of Cardinals on the topic of family life, which took place February 20–21, 2014, in Vatican City.

17. Ibid., 25.

18. Ibid., 26.

19. Ibid.

20. Ibid.

21. Ibid., 29. On this point, see the work of the distinguished Catholic jurist John T. Noonan Jr., *Persons and Masks of the Law: Cardozo, Holmes, Jefferson, and Wythe as Makers of the Masks* (Berkley, CA: University of California Press, 2002). Noonan writes that a legal process "is rightly understood only if rules and persons are seen as equally essential components, every rule depending on persons to frame, apply, and undergo it, every person using rules. Rules and persons in the analysis of law are complementary. By the same token, the paradigm of the impartial judge and the paradigm of the personally responsible judge are equally necessary." Ibid., 18.

22. Kasper, *Gospel of the Family*, 30.

23. Ibid., 31.

24. Ibid., 32.

25. Ibid.

26. See, e.g., Samuel Gregg, "Cardinal Kasper, Communion, and Divorce—Again," *Catholic World Report*, June 4, 2014, http://www.catholicworldreport.com/Item/3173/cardinal_kasper_communion_and_divorceagain.aspx; "Cardinal Caffarra Expresses Serious Concerns about Family Synod Debates," *Zenit*, March 24, 2014, http://www.zenit.org/en/articles/cardinal-caffarra-expresses-serious-concerns-about-family-synod-debates; Robert Spaemann, "Divorce and Remarriage," *First Things*, August/September 2014; John Corbett, OP et al., "Recent Proposals for the Pastoral Care of the Divorced and Remarried: A Theological Assessment," *Nova et Vetera* 12, no. 3 (2014): 601–30.

27. Kasper, *Mercy*, 179.

28. As this project progresses, I look forward to delving more deeply into comparative legal studies, in order to see how the legal systems of other countries address the questions I treat below.

29. The definition of "adultery" in the *Catechism of the Catholic Church* focuses upon the sexual component of the act. Yet there is precedent in both the Catholic moral tradition and in the legal traditions of the West for the developments of more nuanced understandings of the wrong targeted by specific moral prohibitions. We no longer view adultery as a property crime, for example.

30. See, e.g., James Fitzjames Stephen, *A History of the Criminal Law of England* (London: Macmillan,1883). For a brief overview, see Charles E. Moylan Jr., "A Brief History of Criminal Homicide and Its Exponential Proliferation," Maryland Institute for Continuing Professional Education of Lawyers (2002). For an account of how factors that initially triggered a sovereign's pardon (a concept related to but not identical with mercy) were incorporated into nuanced systems of justice, see Kathleen Dean Moore, *Pardons: Justice, Mercy, and the Public Interest* (New York: Oxford University Press, 1997).

31. William H. Theis, "The Double Jeopardy Defense and Multiple Prosecutions for Conspiracy," *Southern Methodist University Law Review* 49 (January–February 1996): 269–307. See also Jeffrey M. Chemerinsky, "Counting Offenses," *Duke Law Journal* 58 (2009): 709–46, to whom these examples are indebted.

32. Theis, "Double Jeopardy Defense," 280, citing Commonwealth v. Robinson, 126 Mass. 259 (1879) (keeping a tavern is a single continuing offense).

33. Ex Parte Snow, 120 U.S. 274 (1887); see Theis, "Double Jeopardy Defense," 280–81.

34. Ex Parte Nielsen, 131 U.S. 176 (1889); see Theis, "Double Jeopardy Defense," 280–81.

35. There is a separate question about the status of the second marriage, as legitimating sexual activity. Fully addressing this question

is beyond the scope of this paper. I think it is possible to say that after a civil divorce from a sacramental marriage, it is possible for a man or woman to enter into a new, natural (not sacramental) marriage, in which a sexual relationship is morally permissible.

36. See the helpful analysis in Jeffrey R. Boles, "Easing the Tension between Statutes of Limitations and the Continuing Offense Doctrine," *Northwestern Journal of Law & Social Policy* 7 (Spring 2012): 291–56. I am deeply indebted to his article for both his own insights and his valuable collection of sources and citations, which I draw upon below.

37. United States v. Yashar, 166 F.3d 873, at 875 (1999), quoting Toussie v. United States, 397 U.S. 112 at 122.

38. United States v. McGoff, 831 F.3d 1071, 1079 (D.C. Cir. 1987).

39. Boles, "Easing the Tension," 225.

40. Toussie v. United States, 397 U.S. 112 (1970).

41. As the Toussie dissent notes, most courts had previously considered draft evasion to be a continuing offense.

42. Boles argues that the Toussie test should be refined to direct courts to investigate whether each element of the crime continuously causes harm. Boles, "Easing the Tension," 253–55.

43. United States v. Garcia, 854 F.2d 340, at 343, (quoting Parnell v. Superior Court, 173 Cal. Rptr. 906, 915 [Cal. Ct. App. 1981]).

44. As Bole notes, not all lower courts have applied the Toussie test in this manner; see his essay for an account of cases taking the less adequate approach.

45. United States v. De La Mata, 266 F.3d 1275 (11th Cir. 2001).

46. Ibid., at 1289.

47. In fact, modern case law dealing with bigamy appears to be moving in that direction. In 1991, a military court found that bigamy was not a continuing offense. "We hold that, under the allegations contained in the pleadings of the case, the bigamy

offense…is not a continuing offense." United States v. Lee, 32 M.J. 857 (1991). Instead it was an offense that took place at the time the second marriage was solemnized. Most American states also do not treat bigamy as a continuing offense. See, e.g., People v. Hess, 146 N. Y.S.2d 210, 211 (1995), where the New York appellate court held that "bigamy is not a continuing offense; the crime is committed the instant the second ceremonial marriage is consummated." Consequently, the court held that "a person is not guilty of bigamy because he lives in this state with the partner to an illegal second marriage contracted elsewhere."

48. The key Synoptic texts are Matt 5:31–32 and Luke 16:18 (the Q tradition), and Mark 10:2–12. See also 1 Cor 7:10–11. (My biblical quotations are taken from the English New Revised Standard Version of the Bible.) I am indebted to John P. Meier, *A Marginal Jew: Rethinking the Historical Jesus,* vol. 4, *Law and Love* (New Haven, CT: Yale University Press, 2009). His bibliography is exhaustive.

49. Meier, *Law and Love*, 126.

50. Ibid., 106.

51. Ibid., 110.

52. Meier believes that this contest story is "a literary and theological creation of Mark, welded together out of various traditions and motifs and shaped by Mark's theological agenda and literary style." Meier, *Law and Love*, 123.

53. John T. Noonan Jr., *Power to Dissolve: Lawyers and Marriages in the Courts of the Roman Curia* (Cambridge, MA: Belknap Press, 1972), 404.

5. THE FUTURE OF THE FAMILY FROM A CHRISTIAN PERSPECTIVE

1. In the following, I take many things from Walter Kasper, "Zur Theologie der christlichen Ehe," (1997), in *Die Liturgie der*

Kirche, WKGS 10 (Freiburg i. Br., 2010), 453–519 (*The Theology of Christian Marriage* [Sal Terrae: Santander, 2014]); Kasper, *Das Evangelium von der Familie* (Freiburg i. Br., 2014); (*The Gospel of the Family* [Sal Terrae: Santander, 2014]).

2. If the difference between sex—biological sex—and gender—its sociocultural translation—becomes a fundamental equality and an arbitrarily configured hetero-, homo-, or transsexual sexuality, this signifies a relapse to a neo-Gnostic soul-body duality that ignores the soul-body unity of the human being and the dignity of corporal sexuality; moreover, it represents a new contempt for the body. Concerning the nondiscrimination and respect for the homosexual orientation, cf. *Catechism of the Catholic Church* 2.357–59. Concerning the whole: Karl Lehman, "Theologie und Genderfragen," in *Zuversicht aus dem Glauben* (Freiburg i. Br., 2006), 63–77.

3. This definition of natural law in the sense of the golden rule is found in the *Decretum Gratiani* (D.1 d.a.c.1), which was normative of the iusnaturalist tradition of the Middle Ages, early modernity, and old Protestantism. Natural law was converted into a detailed code only with the Illustration and with neo-Scholastic philosophy, which depended on the Illustration more than it was aware.

4. Pastoral constitution *Gaudium et spes* 47, 52; John Paul II, Apostolic Letter *Familiaris consortio* (1981) 44.

5. Cf. *Familiaris consortio* 46; cf. also the *Letter of Family Rights*, of the Pontifical Commission for the Family (1983), and the *Compendium of the Social Doctrine of the Church of the Pontifical Council Iustitia et Pax* (2004), 209–54.

6. Cf. the versions in the Synoptic Gospels, the clauses on adultery (Matt 5:32 and 19:9) and the posterior, so-called Pauline privilege, on the basis of 1 Cor 7:12–16. Instructive, exegetically as well as effectively and historically: Ulrich Luz, *Das Evangelium nach Matthäus*, in EKK, vol. 1.1 (Neukirchen-Vluyn: Neukirchener Verlag, 1985), 260–79, and vol. 1.3 (Neukirchen-Vluyn: Neukirchener Verlag, 1997), 89–112.

7. Cf. *DH* 1799.

8. Luther, *Great Catechism,* in BSELK 612; cf. 259. That the act of benediction does not qualify as sacrament is due to a different definition of the concept of sacrament—a problem that also appears in the case of the other sacraments and that basically must be resolved ecumenically.

9. Cf. *DH* 1813–1816.

10. Paul VI, Encyclical *Humanae Vitae* (1968): this is the first doctinal document to develop a personalist idea of matrimony. John Paul II took up the theme in the Apostolic Letter *Familiaris consortio,* "On the Family in the World of Today" (1981) and directed an extensive letter to families for the Year of the Family 1994. Pope Francis has convoked a synod for the years 2014–15 with the theme "The Pastoral Challenges of the Family in the Context of Evangelization." In the Apostolic Letter *Evangelii gaudium* (2013) are contained many important affirmations concerning family pastoral action, above all 66.

11. CIC, can. 1055, in the first section speaks, in the sense of the Council, of "matrimonial alliance"; however, then in §2 it speaks newly of the "matrimonial contract," a concept that the Council conscientiously avoids.

12. Of the whole: Eberhard Schockenhoff, *Chancen der Versöhnung? Die Kirche und die wiederverheiraten Geschiedenen* (Freiburg i. Br., 2011); an aid of great spiritual and pastoral wisdom, along the line of St. Alfonso de Ligorio, is the booklet by Bernhard Häring, *Zur Pastoral bei Scheidung und Wierderverheiratung. Ein Plädoyer* (Freiburg i. Br., 1990). An excellent overview of the earliest discussions, Karl Lehmann, *Gegenwart des Glaubens* (Mainz, 1977), 274–308. My analyses in *Das Evangelium von der Familie* (cf. n1), 54–67, have incited a great discussion, in part polemical, which we can't enter into here. Balanced: Bertram Stubenrauch, "Wiederverheiratete Geschiedene und die Sakramente," *StdZ* 232 (2014): 346ff; Andrea Grillo, *Indissolubile? Contributo al debatito sui divorziati risposati* (Assisi, 2014).

13. Dogmatic Constitution *Lumen gentium* 11; Paul VI, Apostolic Letter *Evangelii nuntiandi* (1975), 58, 71; John Paul II, Apostolic Letter *Familiaris consortio* (1981), 21; 49–64; Encyclical *Redemptoris missio* (1990), 51; *Catechism of the Catholic Church* 1.655–58; Francis, Encyclical *Lumen fidei* 52ff.

14. K. Krämer and K. Vellguth, eds., *Kleine christliche Gemeinschaften. Impulse für eine zukunftsfähige Kirche* (Freiburg i. Br., 2012); T. Knieps and Port Le Roi, ed.s, *The Household of God and Local Households. Revisiting the Domestic Church* (Leuven, 2013). Information about the fundamental historical, juridical-canonical, and theological-pastoral importance in art, "Hauskirche," in *LThK3* 4, 1.217–19.

15. Cf. in depth John Paul II, Apostolic Letter *Catechesi tradendae* (1979) 68.

7. THE HOLY FAMILY

1. Cf. M. Ouellet, *Die Familie—Kirche im Kleinen. Eine trinitarische Anthropologie* (Einsiedeln, 2013).

2. A. M. Rouco Varela, "Die Familie: Leben und Hoffnung für die Menschheit," in *Gott ist treu. Festschrift für Paul Josef Cordes*, ed. R. Buttiglione and M. Spangenberger (Augsburg 2010), 30–45, here 30.

3. W. Kasper, *The Gospel of the Family* (Sal Terrae: Santander, 2014), 28.

4. J. Ratzinger, "Lasst das Netz nicht zerreissen. Ein Wort an die Familien" (Homily on the feast of San Silvestre), 1980.

5. Cf. W. Kasper, *Zur Theologie der christlichen Ehe*, in *Die Liturgie der Kirche. Walter Kasper Gesammelte Schriften*, vol. 10 (Freiburg i.Br., 2010), 453–519 (*Theology of Christian Matrimony* [Sal Terrae: Santander, 2014]).

6. J. Ratzinger, "Zur Theologie der Ehe," *Theologie der Ehe*, in G. Krems and R. Mumm (Regensburg–Göttingen, 1969), 83–115, here 84.

7. Cf. G. Appiah-Kubi, *L'Église, famille de Dieu. Un chemin pour les Églises d'Afrique* (Paris, 2008).

8. Cf. R. Fabris and E. Castelluci, eds., *Chiesa domestica. La Chiesa-Famiglia nella dinamica della missione cristiana. Un profilo unitario a piu voci* (Milan, 2009).

9. J. Ratzinger, *Der Gott Jesu Christi. Betrachtungen über den Dreieinen Gott* (München, 1976), 63.

10. J. Ratzinger and H. U. von Balthasar, *Maria—Kirche im Ursprung* (Einsiedeln, 1997).

11. H. U. von Balthasar, "Die marianische Prägung der Kirche," in ibid., 112–30, here 126.

12. J. M. Lochman, "Das Wunder der Weihnacht," in *Das radikale Erbe, Versuche theologischer Orientierung in Ost und West*, by J. M. Lochman (Zürich, 1972), 263–73, here 273.

13. Benedict XVI, "Homily of the Mass in Altötting" (September 11, 2006), in *Insegnamenti di Benedetto XVI*, vol. 2.2 (Vatican City, 2007), 242–46.

14. Benedict XVI, "Homily of the Mass in the Marian Sanctuary 'Meryem Ana Evi' in Ephesus" (November 29, 2006), in ibid., 710–14.

15 G. Lohfink, *Gottes Volksbegehren. Biblische Herausforderungen* (München, 1998), 259.

16. J. Ratzinger, "Das Geschik Jesu und die Kirche," in *Glaube—Erneuerung—Hoffnung. Theologisches Nachdenken über die heutige Situation der Kirche*, by J. Ratzinger (Leipzig, 1981), 18–27, here 21.

17. St. Augustine, *Sermon* 336.

18. Benedict XVI, "Catechesis in the General Audience of 7 February 2007", in *Insegnamenti di Benedetto XVI* vol. 3.1 (Vatican City, 2008), 166–171, here 169.

19. Cf. Pontifical Council for the Family, ed., *Enchiridion della famiglia e della vita. Documenti magisteriali e pastorali su famiglia e vita 2004–2011* (Vatican City, 2012).

20. Cf. Consilium Conferentiarum Episcoporum Europae, ed., *La famiglia: un bene per l'umanità.* Atti del Forum Europeo Cattolico-Ortodosso Trento, Italy, Dec. 11–14, 2008, Bologna 2009; Pontifical Council for the Family, Pontifical Council for the Promotion of Christian Unity, Department for the Relations of the Patriarchal of Moscow, eds., *Ortodossi e Cattolici insieme per la Famiglia* (Vatican City, 2013).

8. FIVE REMINDERS FROM THE PERSPECTIVE OF THE SHEPHERD OF SOULS

1. For the following, cf. Ch. Schönborn, *Die Freude, Priester zu sein. Exerzitien in Ars*, ed. H. Ph. Weber (Freiburg i.Br., 2011), 144–57 (*The Joy of Being a Priest: In the Footsteps of the Curate of Arles* [Madrid: Rialp, 2010]).

2. Ch. Schönborn, *Vom geglückten Leben*, ed. H. Ph. Weber (Vienna, 2008), 105–6.

3. The complex situation is described by D. Klepp in N. Neuwirth, ed., *Familienformen in Österreich. Stand und Entwicklung von Patchwork- und Ein-Eltern-Familien in der Struktur der Familienformen in Österreich*, Österreichisches Institut für Familienforschung der Universität Wien (Wien, 2011), 73–186. M. Mühl, *Die Patchwork-Lüge. Eine Streitschrift* (Munich, 2011), sustains a critical focus, marked also by his personal experience. The Danish specialist in family therapy J. Juul argues in a rather more nuanced form in, *Aus Stiefeltern werden Bonuseltern. Chancen und Herausforderungen für Patchwork-Familien* (Munich, 2011).

4. The furnished data correspond to those published by the Austrian Office of Statistics from the year 2010: http://www.statistik.at/web_de/statistiken/bevoelkerung/eheschliessungen/index.html. Regarding which, cf. R. K. Schipfer, *Familien in Zahlen 2011. Statistische Informationen zu Familien in Österreich*, Österreichisches Institut für Familienforschung der Universität Wien (Wien, 2011).

5. Regarding which, cf. Department of Family of the Pastoral Categorial of the Archdiocese of Vienna, ed., *Aufmerksamkeiten. Seelsorgliche Handreichung für den Umgang mit Geschiedenen und mit Menschen, die an eine neue Partnerschaft denken*, rev. ed. (Wien, 2011).

6. Numerous initiatives offer aid to children of divorced. As an example for Austria we will mention only the association *Rainbows: Für Kinder in stürmischen Zeiten* (http://www.rainbows.at) and, for Vienna in particular, the Center of Attention for Single Mothers and Fathers of the archdiocese (*Kontaktstelle der Erzdiözese für Alleinerziehende*, http://www.alleinerziehende.at/).

7. Cf. Ch. Schönborn, *Wovon wir leben können. Das Geheimnis der Eucharistie*, ed. H. Ph. Weber (Freiburg i.Br., 2006), 142ff.

10. MATRIMONY

1. Joseph Ratzinger, "Introduction", in *Sulla pastorale dei divorziati risposati* (commentaries on the *Letter to the Bishops of the Catholic Church concerning the Reception of Eucharistic Communion by Faithful Divorced and Remarried*), ed. the Congregation for the Doctrine of the Faith, in *Documenti e Studi* 17 [1998]: 24–25; reprinted later in *L'Osservatore Romano*, December 9, 2011.

2. "Introduction", in *Sulla pastorale dei divorziati risposati*, 27–28.

3. E. Corecco, "Il matrimonio nel nuovo CIC: osservazioni critiche, in *Ius et Communio*, ed. E. Corecco, vol. 2 (Casale Monferrato, 1997), 604, published originally in S. Ghetto, ed., *Studi sulle fonti del diritto* (Padova, 1998), 105–30.